SPATIALITY

Spatiality has risen to become a key concept in literary and cultural studies, with critical focus on the "spatial turn" presenting a new approach to the traditional literary analyses of time and history.

Robert T. Tally Jr. explores differing aspects of the spatial in literary studies today, providing:

- an overview of the spatial turn across literary theory, from historicism and postmodernism to postcolonialism and globalization
- introductions to the major theorists of spatiality, including Gilles Deleuze, Michel Foucault, David Harvey, Edward Soja, Erich Auerbach, Georg Lukács, and Fredric Jameson
- analysis of critical perspectives on spatiality, such as the writer as mapmaker, literature of the city and urban space, and the concepts of literary geography, cartographics and geocriticism.

This clear and engaging study presents readers with a thought provoking and illuminating guide to the literature and criticism of "space."

Robert T. Tally Jr. is Associate Professor of English at Texas State University, USA.

THE NEW CRITICAL IDIOM

SERIES EDITOR: JOHN DRAKAKIS, UNIVERSITY OF STIRLING

The New Critical Idiom is an invaluable series of introductory guides to today's critical terminology. Each book:

- provides a handy, explanatory guide to the use (and abuse) of the term;
- offers an original and distinctive overview by a leading literary and cultural critic;
- relates the term to the larger field of cultural representation.

With a strong emphasis on clarity, lively debate and the widest possible breadth of examples, *The New Critical Idiom* is an indispensable approach to key topics in literary studies.

Also available in this series:

SPATIALITY

Robert T. Tally Jr.

Routledge
Taylor & Francis Group

LONDON AND NEW YORK

First published 2013 by Routledge
2 Park Square, Milton Park, Abingdon, Oxon OX14 4RN

Simultaneously published in the USA and Canada by Routledge
711 Third Avenue, New York, NY 10017

Routledge is an imprint of the Taylor & Francis Group, an informa business

British Library Cataloguing in Publication Data
A catalogue record for this book is available from the British Library

Library of Congress Cataloging in Publication Data
Tally, Robert T.
Spatiality / Robert T. Tally Jr.
p. cm. – (The new critical idiom)
Includes bibliographical references and index.
1. Literature, Modern – History and criticism. 2. Space perception
in literature. 3. Geocriticism. 4. Place (Philosophy) in literature. I. Title.
PN56.S667T35 2012
809'.9332 – dc23   2012017742

ISBN: 978-0-415-66439-4 (hbk)
ISBN: 978-0-415-66440-0 (pbk)
ISBN: 978-0-203-08288-1 (ebk)

Typeset in Garamond
by Taylor & Francis Books

MIX
Paper from
responsible sources
FSC
www.fsc.org   FSC® C004839

Printed and bound in Great Britain by
TJ International Ltd, Padstow, Cornwall

For Paul A. Bové

CONTENTS

SERIES EDITOR'S PREFACE

The New Critical Idiom is a series of introductory books which seeks to extend the lexicon of literary terms, in order to address the radical changes which have taken place in the study of literature during the last decades of the twentieth century. The aim is to provide clear, well-illustrated accounts of the full range of terminology currently in use, and to evolve histories of its changing usage.

The current state of the discipline of literary studies is one where there is considerable debate concerning basic questions of terminology. This involves, among other things, the boundaries which distinguish the literary from the non-literary; the position of literature within the larger sphere of culture; the relationship between literatures of different cultures; and questions concerning the relation of literary to other cultural forms within the context of interdisciplinary studies.

It is clear that the field of literary criticism and theory is a dynamic and heterogeneous one. The present need is for individual volumes on terms which combine clarity of exposition with an adventurousness of perspective and a breadth of application. Each volume will contain as part of its apparatus some indication of the direction in which the definition of particular terms is likely to move, as well as expanding the disciplinary boundaries within which some of these terms have been traditionally contained. This will involve some re-situation of terms within the larger field of cultural representation, and will introduce examples from the area of film and the modern media in addition to examples from a variety of literary texts.

ACKNOWLEDGEMENTS

In exploring theories of spatiality and of literature for many years, I have benefited enormously from the support of numerous friends, colleagues, and teachers. I would especially like to thank Paul A. Bové, to whom this book is dedicated, for his meticulous criticism, generous encouragement, and overall mentorship. I am also indebted to the many other professors who offered guidance along the way, including Jonathan Arac, John Beverley, Lawrence Goodwyn, Sabine Hake, Fredric Jameson, Ronald Judy, Toril Moi, Michael Moses, Valentin Mudimbe, Dana Polan, Rick Roderick, James Rolleston, and Kenneth Surin; each offered valuable comments on papers that, in retrospect, turned out to be early forays into spatiality studies. In recent years at Texas State University, Michael Hennessy and Ann Marie Ellis have been tireless supporters of my work. I am grateful to John Drakakis, who provided detailed, constructive criticism along with his careful editing of the manuscript, and to Niall Slater and Polly Dodson of Routledge for their helpful editorial assistance throughout the process. Finally, I thank the Britches sisters for keeping things lively, and Reiko Graham for her constant enrichment of my lived spaces.

INTRODUCTION

YOU ARE HERE

Beginning as one always does in the middle, *in mediis rebus*, one experiences a sense of disorientation, a sort of cartographic anxiety or spatial perplexity that appears to be part of our fundamental being-in-the-world. It is an experience not unlike that of Dante, in the opening lines of his *Commedia*:

> Midway along the journey of our life,
> I woke to find myself in a dark wood,
> for I had wandered off from the straight path.
>
> (Dante 1984: 67)

As a number of critics and theorists have noted, this bewilderment has increased with the modern and especially postmodern condition, where the traditional signposts or divine guidance are no longer available. As famously summarized by the American critic Fredric Jameson, after describing his own sense of displacement in the *selva oscura* ("dark wood") of the Westin Bonaventure in an infernally postmodern Los Angeles,

> [T]his latest mutation in space—postmodern hyperspace—has finally succeeded in transcending the capacities of the individual human body to locate itself, to organize its immediate surroundings perceptually, and cognitively to map its position in a mappable external world.
>
> (Jameson 1991: 44)

There is something truly terrifying, or at least rather frustrating, in being lost. Not to know where one is, or perhaps, not to know where one is relative to where one would like to be, is a thoroughly unpleasant feeling. In such a situation a sign, any sign, would help, but most useful would be a map. The map is one of the most powerful and effective means humans have to make sense of their place in the world, whether in a wide-ranging and abstract sense of "transcendental homelessness" as Georg Lukács called it (1971: 41) or in the everyday sense of trying to gain one's bearings in a shopping centre or grand hotel. The map offers a fictional or figurative representation of the space in which we find ourselves, and the reassuring "You are here" arrow or dot or other marker provides the point of reference from which we can both imagine and navigate the space.

In a manner of speaking, literature also functions as a form of mapping, offering its readers descriptions of places, situating them in a kind of imaginary space, and providing points of reference by which they can orient themselves and understand the world in which they live. Or maybe literature helps readers get a sense of the worlds in which others have lived, currently live, or will live in times to come. From a writer's perspective, maybe literature provides a way of mapping the spaces encountered or imagined in the author's experience. Completely apart from those many literary works which include actual maps, the stories frequently perform the function of maps. As Ricardo Padrón asks,

> Couldn't we say that these texts themselves, therefore, constitute some sort of map, even if they don't come accompanied by illustrations? After all, they allow us to create mental images of the places they describe, even in the absence of actual illustrations. Not

only do they allow us to picture places and spaces, but by telling stories that take place in them, or by sculpting characters associated with them, they give those places life and meaning. Indeed, any iconographic maps of the worlds imagined by these texts might even miss the point, by reducing their rich engagement with space and place to the fixity of a cartographic image.

(Padrón 2007: 258–59)

Of course, Padrón does not wish to completely elide the distinction between the actual drawn image and the work produced by literary texts, and neither do I. Rather, I am interested in the ways in which literature allows us to engage with our own experience through its own uniquely literary means. Nevertheless, literary cartography, literary geography, and geocriticism enable productive ways of thinking about the issues of space, place, and mapping after the **spatial turn** in literary and cultural studies.

Over the past few decades, *spatiality* has become a key concept for literary and cultural studies. Whereas the nineteenth century appeared to have been dominated by discourses of time, history, and teleological development, and a modernist aesthetic seemed to enshrine temporality as the most important dimension, especially with respect to individual psychology as in Marcel Proust's novel *In Search of Lost Time* or Henri Bergson's philosophy of time and memory. But slowly, and picking up pace especially after the Second World War, space began to reassert itself in critical theory, rivalling if not overtaking time in the significance it was accorded by critics and theorists, who were then more likely to address spatiotemporality or allow space to have a more equal footing with time in their analyses. The "spatial turn," as it has been called, was aided by a new aesthetic sensibility that came to be understood as postmodernism, with a strong theoretical critique provided by poststructuralism, especially in French philosophy, but quickly extending into various countries and disciplines. Moreover, the transformational effects of postcolonialism, globalization, and the rise of ever more advanced information technologies helped to put space in the foreground, as traditional spatial or geographic limits were erased or redrawn. This shrinking of space has been accompanied by a shortening of time, and this "time–space compression," as the British geographer David Harvey has put it (1990: 240–307), is a powerful effect of the modern and postmodern condition. As Jameson has noted, critics and theorists had to develop novel interpretive and critical models to address that "new spatiality implicit in the post-modern" (1991: 418). Today, spatiality has become an unavoid-able, and often extremely valuable, concept for a number of scholars and critics working in contemporary literary studies.

In this book, I endeavour to provide an introduction to spati-ality studies. Spatiality, like temporality, is far too large a topic to be neatly summarized or effectively covered in a single volume. I have chosen therefore to address the topic by focusing almost exclusively on the so-called spatial turn in literary and cultural studies, and even within that discourse my perspective is largely limited to the mapping of social spaces through literature and literary theory, rather than extending the argument to the various ways in which spatiality operates outside of cartography (for example, in geometry or physics) but still affects literary studies. I take mapping to be the most significant figure in spatiality studies today, partly because of its direct applicability to the current crisis of representation often cited by theorists of globalization or postmodernity, but also because of the ancient and well known connections between cartographic and narrative discourse. To draw a map is to tell a story, in many ways, and vice versa.

This book does not attempt to be comprehensive with respect to the creative writers, critics, literary historians, or theorists it covers. Rather, it seeks to make strategic and selective interven-tions into the multilayered and interdisciplinary debates con-cerning space, place, and mapping in literary studies, often focusing primarily on particular writers or texts that I find either representative or especially important to the development of spatiality studies. Of course, as I note in Chapter 2, in this matter of selection and emphasis, I am necessarily following the precepts of narrative and cartography themselves, where one is perpetually plagued with doubt over what to include and what to omit.

To some readers, it might seem odd that this book includes no actual maps, no diagrams, and indeed no illustrations at all. There seems to be a fundamental disconnection in a wholly textual book about mapping, perhaps a bit like Susan Sontag's essay *On Photography* (1977), which notoriously included no actual photographs. But literary cartography or literary geography, as I understand it, operates precisely by virtue of the specifically *literary* nature of the project, and writing itself is a form of spatialization that depends upon the reader's acceptance of numerous conventions. Once actual iconographic diagrams or maps are presented, they become supplemental and sometimes competing images to those conjured forth by the narratives themselves. This is also the case with works of criticism or theory. According to Franco Moretti, for example, Mikhail Bakhtin's essay on the **chronotope** is "the greatest study ever written on space and narrative, and it doesn't have a single map" (Moretti 2005: 35). Nor does Raymond Williams's *The Country and the City* (1973) or Edward Said's *Culture and Imperialism* (1993). This is not to say, of course, that the inclusion of maps or illustrations in a work of fiction, criticism, or theory would diminish its engagement with or effectiveness on matters of spatiality, only that the presence of actual maps is not a requirement for literary cartography, literary geography, or geocriticism.

The quotations from Dante and Jameson at the beginning of this introduction, both of which describe a sense of utter bewilderment in the face of a vast and perhaps unrepresentable spatial array, are possibly confusing in another respect. By juxtaposing the words of a fourteenth-century poem with a consideration of the perplexing new spatiality of the postmodern condition, I have undoubtedly rendered the effect of Jameson's conviction less forceful, and there is a danger of de-historicizing the peculiarities of space, place, and mapping by suggesting that every time one has ever felt anxious in a "dark wood," the experience produces the same sort of cartographic anxiety. As I discuss throughout this book, space and place are indeed historical, and the changing spaces and perceptions of space over time are crucial to an understanding of the importance of spatiality in literary and cultural studies today. However, although spaces and the perception and conception of them vary over time, I maintain that narrative functions as a means of mapping what Edward Soja has referred to as the "real-and-imagined" spaces with which we are so intimately connected (1996), and that the literary cartography produced in narratives then becomes a way for readers to understand and think their own social spaces.

Is Dante's divine *Commedia* then a map? Yes, and in many different ways at once. As Bill Brown has argued, Dante "can respond to his state of bewilderment" in the *selva oscura* ("dark wood") only by attempting to map his position with respect to a much larger geographical, but also spiritual, totality. As Brown observes, Dante responds with "a **cognitive mapping** that unfolds as a guided tour through mythical, religious, and political histories now spatialized within a spiritual cartography which is the poem itself" (Brown 2005: 737–38). Dante not only escapes his initial condition of being lost and disoriented via this grand map and journey through a well ordered "otherworld," but he also establishes for his readers by means of this otherworldly cartography an **allegorical** map by which they may also escape the figurative *selva oscura* in which they find themselves. In this sense Dante's *Commedia* does provide a kind of literary cartography, and readers who study its literary geography can come to terms with the real-and-imagined spaces of their own worlds, worlds that may indeed be far different from the social spaces of *quattrocento* Florence.

As an actual object, as an epistemological device or means of gaining knowledge, as a figurative model, or as a work of art, among innumerable other uses and effects, the map is a powerful force in our lives and the world. As Gilles Deleuze and Félix Guattari point out at the beginning of their ambitious and multilayered philosophical project in *A Thousand Plateaus*,

> The map is open and connectable in all its dimensions; it is detachable, reversible, susceptible to constant modification. It can be torn, reversed, adapted to any kind of mounting, reworked by an individual, group, or social formation. It can be drawn on a wall, conceived as a work of art, constructed as a political action or as a mediation.
>
> (1987: 12)

Such versatility and polyvalence undoubtedly applies to works of literature, criticism, and theory as well, and it is therefore appropriate that different readers might find different strengths and purposes for them.

This book is divided into four main chapters, each dealing with different aspects of spatial practices in literature. After an initial exploration of the spatial turn in literary studies, I devote one chapter each to writing, reading, and the theory and criticism of literature, examining the relations between literature and social space. Then, after looking at the ways that literature, space, and place relate to one another in mostly realistic or mimetic forms, I shift, by way of conclusion, to the otherworldly spaces of fantasy, **utopia**, or science fiction to imagine different spaces that remain part of the important work of spatiality studies.

Chapter 1 examines the broad-based spatial turn in literature, cultural studies, and critical theory. It provides a brief overview of spatiality in history, including the developments of art and mapmaking that introduced **linear perspective** and mathematical projection, thereby transforming the human experience of space. There follows a review of the rise of cartography during the European age of discovery or exploration, and an account of how the concept of space in modern philosophy shifted over time. Drawing upon the developments of nineteenth-century historicism, I examine the ways in which modernism and eventually postmodernism re-evaluated the significance of space and place. The argument outlines the transition from a model for literary and cultural studies in which time is dominant to one where space asserts itself, looking at how representational problems of modernism and postmodernism caused critics to place greater emphasis on spatiality. I will also review some of the work of important theorists of space, such as Michel Foucault, and geographers J.B. Harley, David Harvey, and Edward Soja. Although the approach is interdisciplinary, the main focus is always on the function and effects of spatiality in literary studies.

In Chapter 2, "Literary cartography," I argue that the imaginative writer functions as a kind of mapmaker, and I examine the ways in which narrative especially operates as a form of mapping.

This is the thesis of Peter Turchi's *Maps of the Imagination: The Writer as Cartographer* (2004), for instance, which is not so much a work of criticism or theory as it is a guide for aspiring fiction writers. Drawing on the work of several theorists of narrative or the novel, such as Mikhail Bakhtin, Erich Auerbach, and Georg Lukács, I suggest that the literary author projects a map onto the often chaotic world that the narrative will attempt to represent, offering a figural or allegorical representation that can be used to guide the reader in various ways. This also speaks to an **existential** condition, one of alienation or loss, as analysed by such thinkers as Martin Heidegger and Jean-Paul Sartre. The alienation experienced in attempting to navigate seemingly unrepresentable spaces is addressed by urban planner Kevin Lynch in *The Image of the City* (1960), whose conceptions of **"wayfinding"** and **"imageability,"** along with the theoretical interventions of Louis Althusser and Jacques Lacan, influenced Jameson's ground-breaking notion of cognitive mapping as the most effective means for apprehending and making sense of the postmodern condition. Jameson's concept then suggests ways of reading spaces and of thinking about the relations between narrative and social space.

Chapter 3, "Literary geography," extends the argument of the writer as mapmaker to a more general discussion of spaces and literature, particularly from the perspective of the reader or the critic who must make sense of the literary maps. Specifically, I examine the ways in which literary criticism and history partakes of, and is transformed into, literary geography. In this chapter I examine what the novelist and critic D.H. Lawrence described as the **"spirit of place,"** which he characterizes as an energy that imbues the writer and the literary work, but which I find more closely associated with the sensibilities of the reader. Examining the comments of other novelists, including Virginia Woolf and Umberto Eco, I note that the literary geography is not always as simple as the registration of "real" social spaces in an "imaginary" textual world. Following this, I analyse several different approaches to space and different kinds of place, focusing especially on the nuanced dichotomy of rural and urban spaces. For example, the British literary critic Raymond

Williams's analysis of *The Country and the City* (1973) charts the transformation of these terms, and these spaces, in British literature, and Edward Said has extended Williams's project by engaging in what he calls "a geographical enquiry into historical experience" in *Culture and Imperialism* (1993). The phenomena of metropolitan space and mobility lie at the heart of the theory of the *flâneur*, developed by French symbolist poet Charles Baudelaire and analysed by German literary critic Walter Benjamin, and the experience of "walking in the city" has been further theorized by French historian Michel de Certeau in ways that demonstrate the multiple meanings associated with spatial practices. In this chapter I will also examine the boldly imaginative project of Italian critic Franco Moretti, who aims to replace literary history with a literary geography, partly in an attempt to re-invent the study of literature altogether, as may be seen in such books as his *Atlas of the European Novel, 1800–1900* (1998) and *Graphs Maps Trees: Abstract Models for a Literary History* (2005). I conclude this chapter and my discussion of Moretti's theory of the novel with a consideration of the ways a reader or critic, following Moretti's models, would map the literary text.

I take up the critical theory and practice of "Geocriticism" in Chapter 4, in which I examine the interventions of several influential theorists whose work on space, place, and literature has affected the way scholars approach spatiality studies today. *Geocriticism*, in my use of the term, is flexible enough to encompass such varied work as Gaston Bachelard's poetics of space, Henri Lefebvre's spatial dialectic and production of space, as well as the "new cartography" that Gilles Deleuze declared Michel Foucault to be engaged in. Geocriticism also suggests, somewhat playfully, the spatially nuanced "science" that could supplement and reconstitute the psychoanalytic and phenomenological perspectives seen in such writers as Bachelard, and I have suggested the term *cartographics*, with its somewhat ludic technical sense, gesturing towards something like Louis Marin's *utopics*, in order to suggest the degree to which these critical theories are related to matters of spatiality and mapping. After discussing the phenomenological poetics of space as presented by Bachelard, I examine Lefebvre's provocative and influential theory of the production of space, before tracing the revisionary developments of Foucault's archaeologies and genealogies, as he endeavours to emphasize the spatial character of relations of power/knowledge. I then take up de Certeau's challenge to Foucault's analysis of the **panoptic** relations of power in modern societies, before focusing attention on the often unseen or unacknowledged gendering of social spaces and of geography as a whole. The geocritical discussion of feminist geography suggests the various ways that different spaces are both overlooked and misunderstood. The spatial philosophy of Deleuze, particularly his notions of nomadology and geophilosophy, provide part of the foundation for the geocentric approach to literary studies adopted by Bertrand Westphal. I conclude this chapter with an account of this critical method for reading literary texts and its effects on spatiality studies.

Finally, by way of a kind of open-ended conclusion, I examine the "other spaces" of literature, those which extend beyond realism into the modes or genres of utopia, fantasy, and science fiction. Drawing on Jameson's recent elaboration of a utopianism appropriate to the postmodern condition in the era of globalization, I will discuss the ways that otherworldly literature also helps us to map the real-and-imagined spaces and places of our own world.

1

THE SPATIAL TURN

In a speech given in 1967, the French philosopher Michel Foucault made the following observation, and, in the decades that have followed, more and more critics have come to agree that our own historical moment is somehow the "epoch of space." As Foucault announced,

> [t]he great obsession of the nineteenth century was, as we know, history: with its themes of development and of suspension, of crisis, and cycle, themes of the ever-accumulating past, with its great preponderance of dead men and the menacing glaciation of the world. [...] The present epoch will perhaps be above all the epoch of space. We are in the epoch of simultaneity: we are in the epoch of juxtaposition, the epoch of the near and far, of the side-by-side, of the dispersed. We are at a moment, I believe, when our experience of the world is less that of a long life developing through time than that of a network that connects points and intersects with its own skein.
>
> (Foucault 1986: 22)

Although it would be difficult, and misleading, to identify a particular date or moment when this occurred, a recognizable *spatial turn* in literary and cultural studies (if not the arts and sciences more generally) has taken place. One cannot help noticing an increasingly spatial or geographical vocabulary in critical texts, with various forms of mapping or cartography being used to survey literary terrains, to plot narrative trajectories, to locate and explore sites, and to project imaginary coordinates. A great many literary studies and academic conferences have been devoted to matters of space, place, and mapping, and the spatial or geographical bases of cultural productions have, in recent years, received renewed and forceful critical attention.

A number of factors have contributed to this spatial turn. The French literary critic Bertrand Westphal has suggested that the cataclysmic restructuring of societies during, and in the immediate aftermath of, the Second World War led to the decline in the obsession with time, not to mention the abandonment of the image of history as a progressive movement towards ever greater freedom and enlightenment. He has argued that "[t]he concept of temporality that had dominated the prewar period had lost much of its legitimacy," and "the weakening of traditional historicity, alongside the decoupling of time and progress, has made possible the valorizing rereading of space" (Westphal 2011: 14, 25). Critical theorists, historians, philosophers, and geographers certainly would now hesitate to proclaim much faith in the universal progress of history in the wake of such destruction, and a changing view of temporal movement may have opened the way to those who demanded that greater attention be paid to spatial concerns. Moreover, the postwar era called for a serious rethinking of what had come before, and a number of critics now viewed the pronouncements of the past with renewed scepticism. For example, the social theorists Theodor Adorno and Max Horkheimer examined what they identified as the "dialectic of **Enlightenment**," whereby the most highly valued ideals of the Age of Reason could be shown to have disastrous and barbaric effects (Adorno and Horkheimer 1987). The Marxist geographer Edward Soja points out that the "despatializing historicism" of the late-nineteenth and early twentieth century "occluded, devalued, and de-politicized space" (1989: 4), which effectively meant that the dominant, time-focused discourse of the prewar era served to mask the underlying spatial realities. After the two world wars, these spaces reasserted themselves in critical consciousness.

If the metaphor of time as a smoothly flowing river and the evolutionary theory of history as progressively moving from barbarism towards civilization could not be maintained in the aftermath of concentration camps and atomic bombs, other real historical forces also helped shape the heightened attention to space in the postwar era. Certainly the massive movements of populations—exiles, émigrés, refugees, soldiers, administrators, entrepreneurs, and explorers—disclosed a hitherto unthinkable level of mobility in the world, and such movement emphasized geographical difference; that is, one's *place* could not simply be taken for granted any longer. The traveller, whether forced into exile or willingly engaged in tourism, cannot help but be more aware of the distinctiveness of a given place, and of the remarkable differences between places. The displaced person is understandably more attuned to matters of place, or, as J.R.R. Tolkien once put it in a letter to his son, who was then serving in the Royal Air Force overseas during the Second World War, "I imagine that a fish out of water is the only fish that has an inkling of water" (see Carpenter 2000: 64). This may also be why so many of the twentieth century's great writers (Joseph Conrad, Samuel Beckett, Vladimir Nabokov, to name but a few) were sometimes strangers to the lands and languages in which they wrote. Referring to such writers, the cosmopolitan critic George Steiner has pointed out that "[i]t seems proper that those who create art in a civilization of quasi-barbarism which has made so many homeless, which has torn up tongues and peoples by the root, should themselves be poets unhoused and wanderers across language" (1976: 11). Displacement, perhaps more than a homely rootedness in place, underscores the critical importance of spatial relations in our attempts to interpret, and change, the world.

At the same time, the geopolitical organization and disruptions in the postwar era called attention to the distinctively political essence of geography, as the forces of decolonization, as well as those of neocolonization, made clear that the spaces of the map were not uncontested. The very names by which we knew places such as Rhodesia or Zimbabwe, Burma or Myanmar, were revealed to be matters of immense ideological conflict, and the thoroughgoing intertwinement of history and geography in such contested regions brought home to many the vast inaccuracies and omissions caused by the previous neglect of spatiality or spatial relations in earlier scholarship and theory. For example, the French historian Fernand Braudel's massive study entitled *The Mediterranean* employed what he called "geohistory" to emphasize the "history of man in his relationship to his environment" (1972: 20), and the reassertion of space as a concern in the human sciences has transformed our understanding of social history and criticism. Similarly, greater attention has been paid to spatial organization *within* societies, including the purported divisions between rural and urban, and this has emphasized the degree to which geography conditions even the most mundane aspects of everyday life. The rapid industrialization of the so-called Third World, combined with, and, of course, closely related to, the apparent de-industrialization of the First World, has transformed both the geographical spaces and the ways in which such spaces are understood. The various phenomena and effects often brought together under the label *globalization* have contributed mightily to the spatial confusion, which makes the clarifying overview afforded by mapping and other spatial practices all the more desirable.

Added to this increased mobility and geographic anxiety were revolutionary technological advances that served to suppress distance while also augmenting one's sense of place or of displacement. What the railways, the steam engine, and the telegraph did to nineteenth-century space and time, air travel, telephones, television, and eventually space travel and orbiting satellites, computers and the Internet did to spatiotemporal perception in the twentieth and twenty-first centuries. All of this contributes both to the consciousness of one's place (i.e. one's sense of situatedness in space, as well as of spatial divisions, partitions, and borders) and to the almost unconscious overcoming of place via supersonic travel, synchronic telephone communication, or World Wide Web connectivity around the globe. The mass media's apparent saturation of society, as well as the permeation of almost every nook and cranny of the world by market forces or capitalism, has enhanced what the British geographer David Harvey views as the "time–space compression" in modern and postmodern societies, in which the processes of capitalism "so revolutionize the objective qualities of space and time that we are forced to alter, sometimes in quite radical ways, how we represent the world to ourselves" (1990: 240). By the end of the millennium, it was possible to sense all the more strongly the truth of Karl Marx and Friedrich Engels's poetic observation that, with the constant revolutionizing of social conditions, "All that is solid melts into air" (1998: 54).

Facing such transformations in the so-called "real" world, artists and thinkers have responded in various ways, but one of the most significant and most recent controversial developments is the emergence of *postmodernism*. Postmodernism has been viewed as an aesthetic movement in art, architecture, and literature, and it has also been characterized as a historical period, a new way of thinking, or, in the American critic Fredric Jameson's words, a "cultural dominant" (1991: 4). Sometimes conflated with postmodernism, perhaps owing to the influence of Jean-François Lyotard's book, *The Postmodern Condition* (1984), is poststructuralism, a predominantly French philosophical movement which, continuing a tradition of anti-foundationalism and radical scepticism associated with Friedrich Nietzsche (1844–1900) in the late nineteenth century, called into question not only those "truths" that had formerly been considered unassailable, but also the very means of arriving at truth at all: including the methods of philosophy, history, science, and geography. Just as philosophers like Michel Foucault, Jean-François Lyotard, Jacques Derrida, and Gilles Deleuze have provided innovative critiques of the traditional ways of understanding ourselves and our world, so geographers like Harvey, Soja, and J.B. Harley took their arguments seriously, reimagining their own fields and their ways of looking at society even as they felt empowered to consider more carefully the spatial dimensions of critical social theory. Postmodernism allied to poststructuralism, along with other related discourses, have together been instrumental in effecting this spatial turn. As the British cultural geographer Denis Cosgrove has put it,

> A widely acknowledged "spatial turn" across arts and sciences corresponds to post-structuralist agnosticism about both naturalistic and universal explanations and about single-voiced historical narratives, and to the concomitant recognition that position and context are centrally and inescapably implicated in all constructions of knowledge.
>
> (Cosgrove 1999: 7)

Faced with what Jameson has called "that new spatiality implicit in the postmodern" (1991: 418), literary scholars, social theorists, and cultural critics have given pride of place to spatiality in their researches.

Of course, the experience of space and place, the desire or need for mapping, and the self-conscious reflection on ways and means of achieving a more liveable sense of place, or a better map, are nothing new in human history. To the extent that human beings are "social animals"—Aristotle's *zoon politikon*—they are also *spatial* animals, as well as animals that build things and tell stories. Yet the transformations of social space, which like history itself is a human endeavour but which is not made under circumstances directly chosen by its "makers" (see Marx 1963: 15), affect the ways in which humans operate in space, "use" space, and make sense of their various spatial and social relations. This changing role of spatiality in human history has real consequences for theory and practice. The spatial turn in modern and postmodern literary theory and criticism is an acknowledgement of the degree to which matters of space, place, and mapping had been under-represented in the critical literature of the past. The writers, critics and theorists whose work has directly or indirectly engaged with such matters in recent years attempt not only to remedy this former oversight, but to propose novel ways of seeing a world in which many of the former certainties have become, at the very least, uncertain. The spatial turn is thus a turn towards the world itself, towards an understanding of our lives as situated in a mobile array of social and spatial relations that, in one way or another, need to be mapped.

HISTORICAL PERSPECTIVES

Although recent decades have witnessed a "reassertion of space in critical social theory" (Soja 1989), as well as a "spatial turn" in literary and cultural studies, it should not be forgotten that space has a much more extensive history. In a rather obvious sense, space has always existed, but I am interested in how literary cartography emerges and functions to make sense of the world in novel ways. In the next chapter, I will discuss in more detail the ways in which ancient and modern literature offered literary cartographies of the world system as their authors imagined it. Here I will examine one radical alteration in the way that space was perceived, before describing some of the developments in spatiotemporal theory that led up to the "spatial turn" in twentieth-century literary and cultural studies. This spatial turn is best understood as a re-emergence of spatiality in critical thought, for the history of perceptions of space and time from the early modern era to the present reveals a waxing and waning of spatial pre-eminence. It will help, therefore, to put things into some sort of historical perspective.

In the Renaissance or early modern period, several fundamental changes to the way the world was imagined occurred, and these had lasting consequences which would come to determine our own views in the twenty-first century. Among the most radical, perhaps deceptively so, was the development of linear perspective, which not only enabled more "accurate" pictorial representations in the visual arts but also occasioned a wholesale re-imagining of space and of human spatial relations. This is a crucial moment in the history of spaces. To the common-sense point of view, the idea that space and its perception even *has* a history might seem eccentric. After all, surely human beings equipped with eyes, as well as the other sensory organs, have always had the physical means to experience space and place in more-or-less the same way? Yet the historical record discloses that people of different cultures and at different times have indeed perceived space differently, and the developments of new "ways of seeing," to use the English art critic John Berger's phrase, radically alter our experience of space and place.

An interesting case in point can be found precisely in the development of linear perspective in art, architecture, and more generally the representation of reality itself. The American scholar Leonard Goldstein has argued persuasively that the development of linear perspective between the thirteenth and fifteenth centuries is "a mode of representation specific to capitalism at a particular stage of its development" (1988: 135). As Goldstein sees it, space when ascertained according to linear perspective has three key aspects: (1) space is continuous, isotropic, and homogenous; (2) space is quantifiable; and (3) space is perceived from the point of view of a single, central observer. Goldstein goes on to argue that the emergence of early capitalist forms of private property and commodity productions entailed, or perhaps *required*, new ways of seeing space (1988: 20–21). Space could now be measured, divided, quantified, bought and sold, and above all controlled by a particular individual who, in theory, could be the sovereign ruler of all he surveyed. The relatively sudden shift from the more two-dimensional iconographic images of the Middle Ages and the deeper, more geometric three-dimensional drawings of the Italian Renaissance reflected radical revisions to the customary ways of interpreting the world. In other words, it is not that the physical world or human binocular vision had changed, but that the newly forged social relations in the early modern period called for new ways of seeing.

> But the new point of view, which includes linear perspective and mechanism as its method of investigation, is superior [to the earlier, iconographic mode] since it gives people a greater control over their environment, both physical and social, than previous interpretations of the world. The new, to put it a little differently, is the response to major changes in the social structure for which the old solutions are no longer adequate.
>
> (1988: 151)

As Goldstein concludes, "[l]inear perspective, then, is an interpretation of the world" (1988: 151). Moreover, by positioning the viewer at a particular point in space, linear perspective also makes possible a new image of the individual. Although this is not quite the same as the bourgeois "individualism" that appears at a later stage of modernity, this is clearly the beginning of a process that will culminate in the identification of the individual subject as the locus and source of meaning.

The art historian Samuel Y. Edgerton has also argued that the development of linear perspective in the Renaissance was closely related to material changes in the social sphere. Edgerton points out that the discovery of the New World disrupted the older, medieval view of space, which had drawn from an Aristotelian view of spaces as finite and discontinuous. "Finally, in the fifteenth century, there emerged mathematically ordered 'systematic space,' infinite, homogeneous, and isotropic, making possible the advent of linear perspective" (1975: 159). Edgerton goes on to note that the development of linear perspective in art, and especially in science or technology, went hand in hand with another technological breakthrough, the printing press:

> It should not be overlooked that almost coincidental to the appearance and acceptance of linear perspective came Gutenberg's invention of moveable type. Together these two ideas, one visual, the other literary, provided perhaps the most outstanding scientific achievement of the fifteenth century: the revolution in mass communication. Linear perspective pictures, by virtue of the power of the printing press, came to cover a wider range of subjects and to reach a larger audience than any other representational medium or convention in the entire history of art. It is fair to say that without this conjunction of perspective and printing in the Renaissance, the whole subsequent development of modern science and technology would have been unthinkable.
>
> (Edgerton 1975: 164)

Combined with this revolution in media, other technological developments in the early modern epoch altered the way people perceived and experienced space. Astronomy and geometry would offer new means of coordinating the immediately perceived data of everyday life with the supra-individual forces of the cosmos, and devices like the sextant, the compass, or later the telescope would allow, and indeed require, space to be imagined differently.

THE RISE OF CARTOGRAPHY

It is not surprising that such important developments in geometry, art, architecture, and cartography should emerge in the so-called "Age of Discovery," a period during which the **orientation** of European thought changed entirely, both literally and figuratively. The very word "orientation" means "facing east," and the supplementary meaning that this term retains today, that is "to get one's bearings" or "to understand one's place," made sense for medieval Europeans who derived their sense of place in the world relative to the Holy Land to the East and, in particular, to Jerusalem. Medieval cartography, exemplified in the form of the *mappamundi*, combined religious instruction and geographical information, as "the geographical 'facts' of the classical heritage were now transformed to give them a Christian meaning. For example, the traditional eastern orientation of the map now gained new significance by the presence of the Garden of Eden in the east" (Edson 2007: 15). By the late fifteenth century, however, the dominant worldview afforded by such an orientation was becoming less tenable. The oldest extant terrestrial globe, the *Erdapfel* (or "earth-apple") of the Renaissance German geographer Martin Behaim, was constructed in 1492, a year in which the world as imagined by Europeans would begin to look quite different.

As a philosophical matter, the globe became another way of attaining a "God's-eye-view," now of the entire planet. For example, it was no longer possible to regard the old medieval **T-and-O maps** as reflecting a credible divine plan (see Edgerton 2009: 12–13). In those models, the *orbis terrarum* was depicted as a circle with a horizontal line across the centre and a vertical line midway through the lower half, completing the T and effectively dividing the world into its three continents: Asia, Europe, and Africa. As with other medieval maps, Asia is on top since the orientation of maps were to the East, so Jerusalem represented the centre of the T's crossbar and hence the centre of the world itself. But the globe presented a different image, and with the technological development of the compass, magnetic north became the means of orientation for mapmakers. Further, the discovery of the Americas required that many patterns of this religious worldview had to be reconfigured.

Notably, however, such patterns were not entirely abandoned, as we can see in several centuries' worth of efforts by explorers and cartographers to square the circle of physical reality and divine order, which led to maps that sometimes depicted imaginary lands, such as the *terra australis incognita*, as a way of producing the desired symmetry. Some early modern maps went so far as to include this or that Biblical place, locating the Garden of Eden in South America, for example. But in the aftermath of the voyages of Christopher Columbus at the end of the fifteenth century, spatial relations and perceptions could no longer remain the same, and overtly theological presentations of the world's spaces became less prevalent. As Edson observes, "[w]hen the earthly paradise no longer appears on the world map, we have a new mapping tradition, more devoted to the physical measure of space than to its transcendent, theological meaning" (Edson 2007: 15).

The sheer volume of geographic data returning to Europe in the ships of Columbus, Vasco da Gama, Amerigo Vespucci, Ferdinand Magellan, and others must have utterly astonished and inspired the thinkers of the era. Of course, the gold, silver, spices, and human cargo in those ships also did their part to transform European societies. In Thomas More's *Utopia*, the satirically ideal island counterpart to England was actually discovered on one of Vespucci's voyages, and, in a kind of dialectical reversal of truth and fiction, others followed the letter of text and journeyed to the Americas in search of Utopia. For instance, in 1693 Cotton Mather wrote that, while searching for More's imaginary island, some of the puritans "might now have certainly found a Truth in their Mistake," for "*New England* was a true *Utopia*" (1862: 12). Unlike Vespucci's more commercial motives for setting sail, Mather's pilgrims were seeking a religious utopia, and it is worth remembering that More's 1516 *Utopia* was also published on the

eve of a religious revolution in Europe, as the Protestant Refor-
mation created social, political, and theological upheavals that
reverberated throughout the following century and beyond. In the
wake of the voyages of exploration, the advances in technology,
and the social transformations throughout the continent, it is no
surprise that fifteenth- and sixteenth-century Europe witnessed a
kind of revolution in spatiality.

Columbus, who was after all on an errand to Cathay (China),
had thought that the new world he had discovered was part of
Asia, and thus his geography of the world was updated, but not
transformed. The first world map to use the name *America* for the
new world continents, Martin Waldseemüller's 1507 *Universalis
Cosmographia* also exploded the old tri-continental worldview,
and assimilated a new, "fourth part of the *orbis terrarium* geo-
graphically independent of Asia and Africa and [...] commen-
surate with the traditional three" (Padrón 2004: 20). The image
of the world presented on a map thus brought with it philosophical and ideological reverberations.

At roughly the same time, many European societies were
undergoing internal social transformations, related to, but distinct
from, the overseas explorations. Elsewhere I have discussed three
distinct spatiopolitical ensembles or "zones" emerging in the
Baroque epoch: the *national* (or the space of the state), the *extraterritorial* (the periphery, including colonial spaces), and the *local*
(especially the urban space of the capital); a fourth spatial
ensemble is the *global*, or the space of the world-system (Tally
2009: 12–13). These spaces played off and reinforced one another,
as the centrifugal force of the emerging nation-states which made
possible greater colonization and exploration found its counterpart
in the centripetal force which enabled the increased concentration
of power in the great capital cities, as well as the accumulation *of*
capital in such places. After 1700, we tend to take it for granted
that the modern nation-state, the subject of Thomas Hobbes's
Leviathan (1651), is the principal form of political and economic
organization, but as Carl Friedrich has pointed out, in 1600 the
case was far from certain, since many monarchies attempted to
retain feudal hierarchies and the Counter-Reformation aimed
at reuniting Christianity under one Empire. By the end of the

seventeenth century, however, the modern state form, complete with its "statist" bureaucrats and the new science of "statistics," dominated the political geography of Europe (see Friedrich 1952: 1–3). As noted earlier, these forces shaped, and were shaped by, new configurations and conceptions of space.

One notable development was the emergence of the capital city. Whereas city-states had ancient roots, the new capital city reflected a different spatiopolitical organization. As Lewis Mumford put it, "a change in the entire conceptual framework took place," and, above all, "a new conception of space" (Mumford 1938: 91). In his aptly titled *Europe of the Capitals, 1600–1700*, the great Italian art historian Guilio Carlos Argan explained that:

> The structure of the capital city, determined by the new political function of the State, went far to shape the seventeenth-century conception of space. In the capital city, modern man does not live in familiar, unchanging surroundings; he is caught up, rather, in a network of relations, a complex of intersecting perspectives, a system of communications, a ceaseless play of movements and counter-movements. His position in this articulated space, whose limits are beyond his ken, is at once central and peripheral; similarly, on the "world stage," the individual is at once the protagonist and the supernumerary.
>
> (1964: 37)

Again, the perception and the experience of space combine, not always smoothly, in transforming the geographical reality of human existence, and this has profound effects for the interpretation of that reality.

In *Inventing America*, José Rabasa analyses the allegorical significance of Gerhard Mercator's 1595 *Atlas*, showing how its semiotic system both reinforces and calls into question the Eurocentric worldview (1993: 180–209). Indeed, the worldview established on Mercator's map altered the way we imagine the geopolitical framework of the world. Mercator is perhaps most famous, or notorious, for the **Mercator projection**, a mathematical formula used to solve the problem of depicting round space on a flat map. The first world map using Mercator's projection was Abraham Ortelius's 1564 "mappemonde" (reprinted in his 1570 *Theatrum Orbis Terrarum*), and it shows a grotesquely aggrandized northern hemisphere; the farther away from the Equator, the larger the land appears. Mercator's projection knowingly distorts the actually existing space in order to serve better the needs of navigation. Although its places look oddly out of shape or scale, these maps were useful, as navigators could plot courses using straight lines. I will return to this in later chapters, but for the moment it is worth noting that the deliberately false or *fictional* image of the world in the Mercator map had greater practical value for seventeenth-century sailors than would a more factually accurate chart.

Maps employing Mercator's projection are still used today, as we can see in those depicting Greenland as roughly the same size as South America, whereas, in reality, South America is about seven times larger. Understandably, such maps are controversial, and indeed, Mark Monmonier, in his book *How to Lie with Maps* (1991), has shown how the exaggerated zones served ideological purposes. For instance, during the Cold War, American anti-Communists might enhance their arguments of a Red menace by pointing out how frighteningly large the Soviet Union appeared on their twentieth-century maps. Moreover, as Monmonier points out, even though more accurate "equal-area" map projections had been available since at least 1772, "Mercator's projection provided the geographic framework for wall maps of the world in many nineteenth- and twentieth-century classrooms, and more recently for sets of television news programs and backdrops of official briefing rooms" (1991: 96). The popularity of this image of the world was also undoubtedly the result of some strategic political manoeuvring: "The English especially liked the way the Mercator [projection] flattered the British Empire with a central meridian through Greenwich and prominent far-flung colonies in Australia, Canada, and South Africa" (1991: 96).

It may be surprising to learn that, although some form of mapping has undoubtedly been used throughout human history, what we think of as maps are relatively new. As Tom Conley points out in *The Self-Made Map: Cartographic Writing in Early Modern France* (1996), aside from the **portolan charts** of Mediterranean navigators, which were used to help locate harbours, "at the beginning of the fifteenth century, maps were practically non-existent, whereas only two centuries later they were the bedrock of most professions and disciplines" (1996: 1). Some of the reasons for this rise of cartography, such as the development of linear perspective, the growth in quantitative methods, new world explorations, social reconfigurations, and various technological advances, have already been discussed, but the overall effect of these and other factors is that the map becomes a preeminent form of knowledge and power in the early modern era, and its pre-eminence continues on in twenty-first-century societies.

Today, in the wake of critical theory, we are less surprised to hear that maps, or any "scientific" device or discourse for that matter, are also ideological, that they are imbedded within and often serve the interests of structures of power or domination. But this is partly because the ascension of cartography in the early modern era made the map *the* primary way of viewing the world, which in turn became the mode by which power was exercised in the world. As the geographer J.B. Harley has pointed out in "Deconstructing the Map" (reprinted in Harley 2001) cartography is

> thoroughly enmeshed with the larger battles which constitute our world. Maps are not external to these struggles to alter power relations. The history of map use suggests that this may be so and that maps embody specific forms of power and authority. Since the Renaissance they have changed the way in which power is exercised. In colonial North America, for example, it was easy for Europeans to draw lines across the territories of Indian nations without sensing the reality of their political identity. The map allowed them to say, "This is mine; there are the boundaries." Similarly, in the innumerable wars since the sixteenth century it has been equally easy for the generals to fight battles with colored pins and dividers rather than sensing the slaughter of the battlefield. Or again, in our own society, it is still easy for bureaucrats, developers, and "planners" to

> operate on the bodies of unique places without measuring the social dislocations of "progress." While the map is never the reality, in such ways it helps us to create a different reality.
>
> (Harley 2001: 167–68)

As Harley makes clear, the cartographic revolution of the sixteenth century continues to have lasting effects. Among the most significant is that the view afforded by the map enables one to detach oneself from the phenomena studied, as with the general poring over maps rather than trudging through the battlefields, and this abstraction alters the underlying reality. Further, the imagery on the map projects far more than the pictorial depiction of geographical information. In Joseph Conrad's novel *Heart of Darkness* (first published 1902), for example, Marlowe describes the thrill he felt when looking at the "blank spaces" on his map, especially the central part of Africa, since those were relatively unknown places to be explored. Later, as he looks at a colonial map of the Belgian Congo, Marlowe notices how the blankness has been filled in with "all the colours of a rainbow. There was a vast amount of red—good to see at any time, because one knows that some real work is done in there, a deuce of a lot of blue, a little green, smears of orange, and, on the East Coast, a purple patch to show where the jolly pioneers of progress drink the jolly lager-beer" (1969: 11, 14–15).

In "Geography and Some Explorers," Conrad ridiculed the "fabulous geography" of the Age of Discovery, which had filled in the unexplored spaces with sea monsters and other fanciful illustrations, preferring the "blank spaces" of "honest" modern maps: "From the middle of the eighteenth century on, the business of mapmaking had been growing into an honest occupation registering the hard won knowledge but also in a scientific spirit recording the geographical ignorance of its time" (1921: 19). The scientific advances in cartographic practices are also related to a revolution in modern thought, and the novel conceptions of space in modern philosophy and science are closely connected to the abstract thinking associated with the geometric method, in which space is no longer, or not necessarily, tied to place.

SPACE IN MODERN PHILOSOPHY

Many of the advances in art, architecture, urban planning, and geography involved the increased attention to geometry, and modern philosophy took its cue from mathematics in reimagining the world. It is no mere coincidence that "the founder of modern philosophy," as he is widely considered (see Russell 2004: 511), was also a mathematician and the inventor of analytic geometry. Indeed, one might say that René Descartes (1596–1650) based his entire philosophical system on a mathematical, and spatial, principle, the Archimedean point. In his second meditation, Descartes explains that "Archimedes used to demand just one firm and immovable point in order to shift the entire earth; so I too can hope for great things if I manage to find just one thing, however slight, that is certain and unshakeable" (Descartes 1996: 16). The one thing, of course, will be the Cartesian first principle, *Cogito ergo sum* ("I think, therefore I am"), the foundation upon which Descartes erects his philosophy and science. It is worth noting that this principle already involves a particular point of view, an individual perspective that can somehow be extrapolated into a larger vision of the world as a whole. In this respect, the beginnings of modern philosophy are at home in the new space opened up in late Renaissance or Baroque epochs.

A proper discussion of the concept of space in modern philosophy would take us far beyond our main concern with the spatial turn in literary and cultural studies. However, a brief examination of the popular, though contested, conceptions of space in seventeenth- and eighteenth-century philosophy can help to explain why, as Foucault put it, history, not geography, was "the great obsession of the nineteenth century."

Descartes maintains a notion of Euclidean space in which space cannot be separated from the bodies *in* space. Following the Aristotelian definition, the term *body* here refers to anything with mass and dimensionality, and for Descartes all bodies have a fundamental characteristic, spatial extension, so that what we think of *as* space is really just this extension of bodies. For example, a bottle may be filled with water, but when it is empty, it is still filled with air. In a sense, then, there is no empty space because it is full of bodies. Traditionally, space was understood either as a plenum that was full of matter, as in the theory of a classical atomist like Lucretius (circa 99–55 BCE), or a vacuum that could be completely empty, which was a view Sir Isaac Newton would embrace. Descartes undermines this distinction by focusing on bodies-in-space rather than space itself, and in this conception there can be no space that is separate and distinct from bodies. This space is also full, not because it is an empty container that has been filled with bodies, but because the bodies in space are *part of* space. Cartesian space is fundamentally grid-like, and the geometrical coordinates indicate the part of that space that is a given body or bodies. One can easily see the overlapping influences of art, architecture, mathematics, and philosophy in this view and in the societies of early modern Europe.

Sir Isaac Newton (1642–1727) disagreed with Descartes's argument that space was itself a substance. "Space is, in Newton's view, essentially an absolute, independent, infinite, three-dimensional, eternally fixed, uniform 'container' into which God 'placed' the material universe at the moment of creation" (Ray 1991: 99). Although the debate would continue throughout the eighteenth century, the Newtonian conception generally held sway, at least until Albert Einstein (1879–1955) and the theory of relativity. However, one important objection to the Newtonian conception of space as a container *and* to the Cartesian view of space as matter itself came from the German philosopher Gottfried Leibniz (1646–1716). Leibniz dismissed the notion of absolute space and posited that space is fundamentally relational, that space in and of itself does not really exist at all; rather, space is the *relation* between bodies, just as we might think of "distance" as a relation between two points. In addition, Leibniz saw time as the mere relation between events, and not a thing that exists. Newton had viewed time, like space, as absolute, as indeed had Descartes, but for the most part he limited his discussion to space. Part of Leibniz's objection is theological, since Newton's conception of space as an empty container later filled by God would logically mean that space (and time) existed before creation itself. Still another view was offered by the Dutch philosopher Benedict Spinoza (1632–1677), which effectively held that space *is* God or Nature (*Deus sive Natura*). I shall return to Spinoza in Chapter 4, since his philosophy provides an important foundation for Gilles Deleuze's concept of nomadology.

In *The Critique of Pure Reason*, the German philosopher Immanuel Kant (1724–1804) attempted to resolve the problem, or perhaps to avoid it altogether, by establishing space and time as pure concepts or categories in which every other concept is situated. That is, when we perceive something, it appears to us as already in time and space; time and space are not additional things to be perceived. In his "Copernican Revolution" in thought, Kant hypothesized that our human reason cannot perceive the world as it really is, but only as it is perceived by us. As Kant had noted in an earlier work,

> *Space is not something objective and real*, nor is it a substance, nor an accident, nor a relation; it is, rather, subjective and ideal; it issues from the nature of the mind in accordance with a stable law as a scheme, as it were, for co-ordinating everything sensed externally.
>
> (Kant 1992: 397)

Kant's objects that "most geometers, following the English" who view space "as an *absolute* and boundless *receptacle* of possible things" invoke a conception of space that "belongs to the world of fable." But he also finds that the view of space as a mere relation between actual things, "an opinion which most of our own [i.e., German] people, following Leibniz, maintain," is "in headlong conflict with the phenomena themselves," and its proponents are guilty of a rank empiricism that would "cast geometry down from the summit of certainty" (1992: 397). Contrary to Descartes's and Newton's absolute space, as well as to Leibniz's relational space, Kantian space is a mental construction.

The view of space as a "container" in which things are situated, a mere "relation" between things, or as a "subjective" condition of perception tends to diminish the importance of spatiality, since the philosophical focus turns to the things themselves which are situated in space, or which define the "space," or to the individual perceiving them. Kant's relegation of space to a subjective condition imposed upon the perceived phenomena by the mind offers a way to understand one's relationship with spatiality, but it does not alter the fundamental importance of space. Even in Kant's philosophy, space remains a mere backdrop behind whatever phenomena are really significant. Temporality takes on greater importance as the themes of development, maturation, or a gradual movement over time come to dominate philosophical discourse at the end of the eighteenth century. In the social sphere, geography too moves into the background, as historical processes take centre stage. Of course, the physical features of geography are crucial to history, but in a great deal of nineteenth-century thought, as Foucault had suggested, space appeared to matter only as the location where historical events unfolded. The flow of time and the movement of history by this point came to assume a primary importance.

THE RETURN OF HISTORY

It is not really accurate, however, to say that history *returned* in the late eighteenth century, but one could argue that the events of that era placed history squarely in the foreground, and the philosophical discourse of modernity took shape, at least in part, as a meditation on the historical nature of mankind. In his famous answer to the question, *Was ist Aufklärung?* ("What is Enlightenment?"), Kant announced that "Enlightenment is man-kind's emergence from his self-imposed immaturity" (1963: 3, translation modified). For Kant, the enlightened thinker of the present age had grown up, become an adult, and taken responsibility for his own knowledge, rather than allowing others, such as the medieval Church, to direct and control thinking. By this analogy, Kant indicated that what had come before was a kind of philosophical childhood, and a process of maturation had led to this historical moment.

Earlier thinkers had underscored the significance of historical development. History had long been studied and valued, but the emerging philosophies of history sought to produce theories of historical development that might approximate the certainty of physical laws of Nature. Other philosophers delved into history in search of keys to the present. One important development in this process was the disciplinary practice of philology, or the historical study of language, which took the concept of evolutionary change as its starting point. The Italian philosopher Giambattista Vico (1668–1744) employed a philological analysis in his *New Science* in order to show how *il mondo della nazione* ("the world of nations") developed over time. In Germany, the investigations of Johann Gottfried Herder (1744–1803) into the origin of languages provided a foundation for historicism: the view that works must be understood in their historical context. He also promoted nationalism by advancing the notion that each language represented a "nation" of its speakers. As Benedict Anderson has noted, the rise of philology, combined with the dominance of vernacular tongues over the older, sacred languages of Latin, Greek, or Hebrew, was a key element in the formation of European nationalisms (1991: 70–71). Through history and language, it was thought, a people could discover who and what they were.

The most formative and significant event of this period was the French Revolution of 1789, from which subsequent revolutionaries took their example. For many Europeans, the Revolution portended the dawn of a new age of history, and the past could be reinterpreted in the light of this to show how the historical trajectory of events had led to this moment, seemingly inevitably. This was how the extremely influential German philosopher G.W.F. Hegel (1770–1831) could come to see the present moment, at the beginning of the nineteenth century, as the "end of History." By this, Hegel did not mean that historical events ceased to occur, of course; he meant that the overarching, grand narrative of history—History with a capital "H"—had reached its apotheosis in the modern world, and that the universal development of mankind had attained its historical (and historicist) objective. With the overthrow of feudal hierarchies and the establishment of the liberal nation-state and civil society, mankind itself had achieved its ultimate historical condition.

Hegel's philosophy of history is thus teleological, designating a particular end (or *telos*, in Greek) and imagining the entirety of human history as a process, with successive stages, leading up to that end. From the philosopher's point of view, only at the end of this historical process can one properly know and assess it, so the end of history is also a prerequisite for Hegel's theory. As he puts it metaphorically in *The Philosophy of Right* (first published in 1821), "The Owl of Minerva spreads its wings only with the falling of the dusk" (1967: 13). Tellingly, perhaps, Hegel had named the successive "realms" of world history Oriental, Greek, Roman, and German, which not only subordinated the real geography of these different places to the universal law of history, but established Hegel's own national time-and-place as the ultimate endpoint of world historical development. That is, Hegel saw his own historical moment and geographical location as the point at which human development culminated. Karl Marx (1818–1883), who was at times both Hegel's most insightful scholar and harshest critic, adopted Hegel's philosophy of history, but argued that the motor of historical development was class struggle rather than the divided individual consciousness in conflict. In this view, the emergence of the modern state and the capitalist mode of production signalled just the latest stage of history. For Marx, the "end of history" would require yet another stage, the establishment of communism or a postnational and postcapitalist realm of freedom. In Marx, as in Hegel, history does not necessarily flow in a straight line, but its processes are logical and knowable, and it has a cognizable destination or end.

The notion of historical progression was especially popular and widespread in the nineteenth century, when the French and industrial revolutions were soon joined by further scientific revolutions. Among them, the findings of geology and palaeontology laid to rest the notion of a Biblical timeline, as apparently antediluvian minerals and fossils were unearthed. Where theologians had attempted to identify a date of creation, sometime within the past 6,000 years, the fossil record showed formations that were clearly much older. A great debate within geology had to do with evolutionary theory, particularly whether formations evolved slowly over time through processes such as erosion or whether they were the results of sudden catastrophes. In biology, Charles Darwin's (1809–1882) theory of natural selection challenged the theories of adaptive evolution, and bastardized versions of these theories quickly found adherents in other, non-scientific domains; for example, the Social Darwinists used the notion of the "survival of the fittest" in arguments against providing aid to the poor. Ethnographers and archaeologists, sometimes operating in conjunction with colonization efforts, discovered extinct civilizations and "primitive" peoples, who could then be studied as if they were living fossils of early Europeans. Again, a Hegelian idea of history makes terms like *primitive* and *modern* fit neatly within one overall historical narrative, but, as Eric R. Wolf has argued persuasively in *Europe and the People Without History* (1997), these categories do not well reflect "the bundles of relationships" that constitute the spatiotemporal processes of human history (1997: 3). The emergence of the historical novel at the beginning of the nineteenth century and the emergence of professional historiography shaped the way in which nations and populations were understood. Underlying these narratives were often theories of history that could be used to explain disparate phenomena in a quasi-scientific manner. Indeed, by the end of the nineteenth century, many thinkers considered a truly scientific history, a history that was as much a science as biology or physics, entirely possible.

Amid these multifarious developments in historical thinking, space was not forgotten. Indeed, the nineteenth-century advances in geography and spatial sciences continued apace. As with Conrad's "map-gazing," the spread and development of imperialism necessitated advances in geographical knowledge and practices, and the advances in geology, geography, surveying, and urban planning were also key elements of nineteenth-century thought. But Foucault's sense that nineteenth-century philosophy had given pride of place to temporality and history is borne out in the vast literature of the era. For the most part, even with the developments in spatial knowledge, space was still viewed by philosophy as static, empty, and mere background to historical and temporal events. At the turn of the century, time trumped space as the main object of fascination for many writers and theorists.

THINGS FALL APART

Modernism, like postmodernism, is probably not a very good term for understanding the diverse artistic and philosophical productions with which it is associated. Any endeavour to definitively characterize modernism is likely to be frustrated, like trying to contain a bead of mercury. Nevertheless, the label helps to name an aesthetic mode or field, if only provisionally. In his authoritative study, *All that is Solid Melts into Air* (1982), Marshall Berman describes the transformative forces of modernity as a "maelstrom," and offers a dialectical view of the mutually reinforcing negative and positive aspects of modernism:

> [T]he social processes that bring this maelstrom into being, and keep it in a state of perpetual becoming, have come to be called "modernization." These world-historical processes have nourished an amazing variety of visions and ideas that aim to make men and women the subjects as well as the objects of modernization, to give them the power to change the world that is changing them, to make their way through the maelstrom and make it their own.
>
> (1982: 16)

Berman notes that a characteristic shared by many modernists is that "they are moved at once by a will to change—to transform both themselves and their world—and by a terror of disorientation and disintegration, of life falling apart" (1982: 13).

The radical transformations associated with modernization are both spatial and temporal, but time seems to be the dominant theme in many modernist works of literature. Perhaps this owes something to the dominance of history in nineteenth-century social theory, or to the nostalgia for the past adopted by so many writers and thinkers in their efforts to deal with the ever-changing present, or to the great anxiety over an uncertain future. The French philosopher Henri Bergson (1859–1941) developed theories of time and memory that proved extremely influential, and Bergsonian thought can be detected between the lines of works by Marcel Proust, James Joyce, William Faulkner, and others. Indeed, Proust's *Remembrance of Things Past* (1913–1927) is a seven-volume novel whose point of departure involves an "involuntary memory" spurred by the taste of a biscuit dipped in tea. The flow of time and the vicissitudes of the unconscious contribute to that archetypically modernist technique, the *stream-of-consciousness*. Temporality, along with a strong sense of the individual's personal development over time, was often the pre-eminent subject of the modernist text.

The work of Sigmund Freud (1856–1939), which may itself be considered a form of modernist literature, emerged at the same time and immediately influenced many writers. In his early research, Freud happened upon what one of his patients called the "talking cure" (2004: 34), initially a method of treatment but then an entire psychological system which he would spend the rest of his life elaborating and refining as psychoanalysis. Psychoanalysis can be viewed as an attempt to map the contours of the human mind, and Freud did use spatial metaphors frequently in his writings. Freudian thought also added a temporal element, as Freud discovered that the repetition of an earlier event at a later time is often at the root of the patient's psychological problem. Thus, an early trauma that was forgotten or "repressed" by the mind lies at the heart of one's current neurotic condition, triggered by a more recent but similarly traumatic, though perhaps seemingly insignificant, event. The psychoanalyst then delves through the narrative of the patient's history, since it is the patient's own words that are being analysed, to uncover a secret. This involved the interpretation of dreams or the analysis of the wording of a joke, exemplary texts for literary studies as well. That psychoanalysis proved useful for both creative writers and literary critics is therefore not surprising.

The intensely individual, psychological perspective in many modernist narratives highlights the concern with the *ego* and with the unconscious processes affecting the human subject's sense of self. These works, though epic in their scope, might be considered spatially circumscribed because of this intense focus on the psychological interiority of the narrator or protagonist. As Jameson has suggested, with modernism,

> the phenomenological experience of the individual subject—
> traditionally, the supreme raw material of the work of art—becomes

limited to a tiny corner of the social world, a fixed-camera view of a
certain section of London or the countryside or wherever.

(Jameson 1991: 411)

In such a narrative, it makes sense that space would appear
less important than time, for in the fluvial metaphor, the
individual's psychological being is caught up in the flow of time,
as it is figuratively embodied in, for example, a stream-of-
consciousness narration. The real and imagined spaces beyond
one's self, while undoubtedly still "out there," are not of primary
concern in many modernist works, although, as I will discuss
further in later chapters, such repressed spatiality is present as a
kind of geopolitical unconscious in many modernist poems and
novels.

This is not to say that modernism is only associated with or
interested in time. Joseph Frank famously postulated that
modernist literature had a "**spatial form**," although his understanding of space was largely limited to a temporal characteristic,
simultaneity. Instead of narrating events in a chronological order,
a modernist novel might, for example, juxtapose elements occur-
ring at the same time, as in a famous scene in Gustave Flaubert's
Madame Bovary (1856), in which descriptions of three different
conversations are interwoven together to create the sense of
simultaneity. Because the novel requires a temporal ordering
requiring the reader to read in a certain order, from beginning to
end, the simultaneity or spatiality is artificially imposed by the
author's decision to break the linear narrative into fragments. In a
work like Joyce's *Ulysses* (1922), readers are called upon to project
a kind of spatial mental image as they put these pieces together,
since "[a]ll the factual background summarized for the reader in
an ordinary novel must here be reconstructed from the fragments,
sometimes hundreds of pages apart, scattered through the book"
(Frank 1991: 19). This spatialization of time in modernist
fiction might be considered an allegorical process not unlike the
"cognitive mapping" discussed in the next chapter.

The phrase *Things Fall Apart*, which is the title of the Nigerian
writer Chinua Achebe's 1958 novel about a tragic hero's difficulty
in dealing with the forces of modernization that affect him, comes

from William Butler Yeats's "The Second Coming" (1920), a modernist poem sounding an apocalyptic theme and written just after the First World War. The modernist experience of time as a descent into chaos, of fragmentation and loss, pervades a number of late nineteenth- and early twentieth-century literary masterpieces, culminating in T.S. Eliot's poem *The Waste Land* (1922), in which the entirety of Western, if not world, civilization appears to be preserved, subsumed, and cancelled out. In the modernists' apparent fascination with time it is also possible to see a profoundly spatial anxiety, as the whirl of temporal flux represented in these texts is equally a bewildering reconfiguration of the problem of spatial location. As things fall apart, traditional landmarks may no longer offer guidance. New forms of mapping are called for to make sense of spatial or geographical place and cultural identity.

THE NEW SPATIALITY IMPLICIT IN THE POSTMODERN

The concepts of the postmodern or postmodernism have always been controversial, and efforts to pin down a meaning have been met at one extreme with horror, distain, and scepticism, and at the other with exuberance and joy. Some have suggested that postmodernism is nothing more than the successor in time to modernism or even romanticism, and no definitions of post-modernism can avoid some overlap with other forms, styles, or periods. Some define the postmodern as a radical break from the modern, as a completely new world in which the old ways of seeing and thinking cannot apply to present problems. Some imagine postmodernism so loosely and so ahistorically that one can speak of *Don Quixote* (1615) or *Tristram Shandy* (1759) as postmodern because their narratives employ metafictional techniques. An important tendency of postmodernism appears to be its tendency towards pastiche, its imitative hodgepodge of elements, which sometimes finds elements of modernism or of the early modern mixed into its form and content. The nonlinearity of its history also seems to typify postmodernism, as may be seen in Ihab Hassan's analysis (1987). Hassan's playfully scientific table of contrasting attributes of modernism and postmodernism, including such gems as modernism's paranoia versus post-modernism's schizophrenia (1987: 92), seems like the result of a diverting game as much as anything. It could also invite a radically transhistorical view of the issue, as some of the attributes of postmodernist fiction could easily be found in ancient litera-ture. Hassan's table also suggests that the distinction between modernism and postmodernism may be largely attitudinal, such that the elegiac tone of modernism is merely replaced by a ludic or playful one in postmodernism, but that the underlying realities are largely the same. However these various characterizations attempt to distinguish or conflate postmodernism with other-*isms*, one aspect that has been repeatedly noted is what Jameson has called "that new spatiality implicit in the postmodern" (1991: 418). The recent spatial turn in literary and cultural studies has, for the most part, been a product of, or response to, the postmodern condition.

A key figure in the development of the conception, who was in part responsible for coining the word "post-modern," was the American poet Charles Olson. As Perry Anderson relates in *The Origins of Postmodernity* (1998), around 1951 Olson "started to speak of a 'post-modern world' that lay beyond the imperial age of the Discoveries and the Industrial Revolution" (Anderson 1998: 7). Olson envisioned a large poetic project, a sort of *Anti-Wasteland* that would move across the whole of "the West" from Homer's *Odyssey* through Dante and Melville up to the American present, and some of this artistic and philosophical argument survived in Olson's *Call Me Ishmael* (1947), an extraordinary study of *Moby-Dick*. Olson placed heavy emphasis on space in his work, and this attention to space was tied to his view of the "post-modern":

> Space is the mark of new history, and the measure of work now afoot is the depth of the perception of space, both as space informs objects and as it contains, in antithesis to time, secrets of a humanitas eased out of contemporary narrows. [...] The *gains* of space are already apparent.
>
> (Olson 1973: 2–3)

With Olson, the turn to postmodernity inevitably occasions a spatial turn.

In an effort to historicize the postmodern and to ground it in a more material reality, a number of critics have made the connection between postmodernity and new forms of economic activity in the past 50 years or so. More specifically, the emergence of "late capitalism," which the German economist Ernst Mandel identified as the most recent phase of capitalist development, has introduced the structural transformations to social and cultural practice that have come to be associated with postmodernism. Hence, Jameson's notion that postmodernism is the "cultural logic of late capitalism" (1991: 1–54), and a crucial feature of late capitalism is globalization. One of the most influential thinkers engaged in the discourse of postmodernism is the British Marxist geographer David Harvey, who has argued that the turning point occurred around 1973, when a global recession forced changes to the old (perhaps modernist?) Fordist model of production, inaugurating the era of "flexible production," which in turn is driven by, and productive of, enhanced financialization and globalization that Harvey identifies as a "sea-change" in capitalist accumulation (1990: 189). He remarks that earlier epochs, like the period between 1890 and 1929, had seen the domination of "finance capital" over traditional commodity production, only to find the situation reversed in a "crash."

> In the present phase, however, it is not so much the concentration of power in financial institutions that matters as the explosion in new financial instruments and markets, coupled with the rise of highly sophisticated systems of financial coordination on a global scale. It is through this financial system that much of the geographical and temporal flexibility of capital accumulation has been achieved.
>
> (Harvey 1990: 194)

These processes have made possible and accelerated that "time–space compression" that typifies human experience in the postmodern condition.

In *Postmodernism, or, the Cultural Logic of Late Capitalism*, at once a synthesis of the competing strands of the postmodernism debates and an exploration of possible directions future work might take, Jameson attempts "to see whether by systematizing something that is resolutely unsystematic, and historicizing something that is resolutely ahistorical, one couldn't outflank it and force a historical way at least of thinking about that" (1991: 418). Jameson's bold thesis is announced in his title, and the notion that the postmodern must be understood in terms of "late capitalism," a stage in which the capitalist mode of production has become truly global. He also insists that post-modernism is not a style but a "cultural dominant: a conception which allows for the presence and coexistence of a range of very different, yet subordinate, features" (1991: 4). Jameson thus avoids the confusions of those who would conflate the postmodern with modernist or romantic precursors, among others. Jameson's use of the term *dominant* draws upon literary critic Raymond Williams's useful distinctions between dominant, residual, and emergent cultural forms; rather than making the dubious claims that one form definitively passes away once another emerges, this formulation allows us to see how, at a given moment, something can be dominant while residual cultural forces still exert their power at the same time as emerging ones appear on the scene (see Williams 1977: 121–27). For Jameson, this means that all those residual modernist elements may be still with us, while the postmodern as a cultural dominant can help us both to explain better the differences between the modern condition and our own and to begin to recognize those emergent forces that are already beginning to transform the world as we experience it today.

One of the chief distinctions noted by Harvey, Jameson, Soja, and others is the new importance of space and spatiality in the postmodern. Jameson argues that the characteristically post-modern "waning of affect" might also be thought of as "the waning of the great high modernist thematics of time and temporality." With a nod to Foucault, or perhaps more so to Henri Lefebvre, the French philosopher and author of *The Production of Space* (1974), Jameson asserts that "our daily life, our psychic experiences, our cultural languages, are dominated by categories of space rather than by categories of time" (1991: 16).

Indeed, the new spatiality of the postmodern is both a product of the processes of globalization that have blurred or collapsed spatial barriers and an engine propelling those processes further. As noted at the beginning of this chapter, our experience of space has been utterly transformed by technological advances like air travel, telecommunications, and especially the Internet, which seems to combine the residual, dominant, and emergent elements of cultural production in hitherto unimagined ways. Harvey points out that the collapsing of spatial barriers has had the effect of enhancing the significance of space, as minor spatial differences assume greater importance in the global competition of flexible accumulation. "As spatial barriers diminish so we become much more sensitized to what the world's spaces contain" (Harvey 1990: 294). Hence, a central paradox:

> [T]he less important the spatial barriers, the greater the sensitivity of capital to the variations of place within space, and the greater the incentive for places to be differentiated in ways attractive to capital. The result has been the production of fragmentation, insecurity, and ephemeral uneven development within a highly unified global space economy of capital flows.
>
> (1990: 296)

For Harvey as for Jameson, this postmodern condition calls for a form of cognitive mapping that will enable us to comprehend and negotiate these postmodern spaces.

In the next chapter I will discuss Jameson's idea of cognitive mapping at greater length, but for the moment I will emphasise that, amid the spatial confusion and anxiety of the present moment, a form of cartography appears to be the only really appropriate aesthetic and political practice for the postmodern condition. As Jameson says, "a model of political culture appropriate to our own situation will necessarily have to raise spatial issues as its fundamental organizing concern," and "the political form of postmodernism, if there is any, will have as its vocation the invention and projection of a global cognitive mapping, on a social as well as a spatial scale" (1991: 51, 54). As Harvey warns, however, this laudable endeavour is fraught with difficulties, since our "mental maps" are subject to "the contradictory pressures that derive from spatial integration and differentiation. There is an omni-present danger that our mental maps will not match current realities" (1990: 305). For this reason, Jameson's concept of cognitive mapping remains provisional, figurative and utopian, but no less necessary as a means of dealing with this new spatiality.

THE SPACES OF LITERATURE

In Thomas Pynchon's 1966 novel *The Crying of Lot 49*, the protagonist Oedipa Maas finds herself entangled within a global conspiracy, bewildered by bizarre characters, and lost in the confusion of competing, often inscrutable interests, all while she is attempting to sort out the complex details of a dead man's estate. At one point, she resolves to reread the will itself in an effort to gain a clearer sense of things, and she imagines herself as a "dark machine in the center of the planetarium" that can "bring the estate into pulsing stelliferous Meaning." She writes the following in her memorandum book: "*Shall I project a world?* If not project then at least flash some arrow on the dome to skitter among the constellations and trace out your Dragon, Whale, Southern Cross. Anything might help" (Pynchon 1966: 82).

"Projecting a world" seems an entirely appropriate phrase for describing the role of literature, and a great many literary works have undoubtedly functioned as imaginary maps, diagrams, constellations, and the like. As a means of understanding the world, literature takes the data of life and organizes it according to this or that plan, which can then aid readers in comprehending and navigating a portion of their own world. This aspect of literature is probably as old as storytelling itself, as with ancient epics and myths that helped listeners and spectators make sense of the mysteries of nature. Yet I agree with Lefebvre, Jameson, and Harvey that the material, historical bases underlying human social relations have also produced different spaces, and that these spaces have had to be addressed in novel ways. With respect to literary and cultural productions, these spaces call for new cartographic approaches, new forms of representation, and new ways of imagining our *place* in the universe. Space, place, and mapping, then, are crucial to literary and cultural studies, just as these concepts and practices are required for living in an ever-changing social and geographical milieu.

The profound changes to our everyday lives in our modern or postmodern condition, many of which are undoubtedly beneficial, but some of which have proved to be of dubious value, have seemed to augur a new world, a "brave new world" (as Miranda in Shakespeare's *The Tempest* declared) that requires new methods of art and analysis to aid our understanding. The spatial turn in literary and cultural studies is both a reasonable response to the perplexities of this condition and a tentative exploration of new spaces and representations. As I mentioned in the Introduction, the "human condition" is often one of disorientation, where our experience of being-in-the-world frequently resembles being lost. Already situated *in medias res*, literary and cultural studies have begun to disclose some of the ways of clarifying these difficulties, and those engaged in "spatiality studies," whether further characterized in terms of *literary cartography*, *literary geography*, or *geocriticism*, may continue to uncover or invent new means of making sense of the ways we make sense of the world. In the following chapter, I discuss some of the ways that literature functions as a form of mapmaking.

2

LITERARY CARTOGRAPHY

In the opening lines of "The Chart," a chapter which the narrator asserts, "[s]o far as what there may be of a narrative in this book," is "as important a one as will be found" in *Moby-Dick* (203), Herman Melville dramatizes the literary cartographic project of that novel.

> Had you followed Captain Ahab down into his cabin after the squall that took place on the night succeeding that wild ratification of his purpose with his crew, you would have seen him go to a locker in the transom, and bringing out a large wrinkled roll of yellowish sea charts, spread them before him on his screwed down table. Then seating himself before it, you would have seen him intently study the various lines and shadings which there met his eye; and with slow but steady pencil trace additional lines over spaces that before were blank. [...]
> While thus employed, the heavy pewter lamp suspended in chains over his head, continually rocked with the motion of the ship, and for ever threw shifting gleams and shadows of lines upon his wrinkled brow, till it almost seemed that while he himself was marking out lines and courses on the wrinkled charts, some invisible pencil was

also tracing lines and courses upon the deeply marked chart of his
forehead.

(Melville 1988: 198)

Here Melville depicts Ahab literally poring over his maps, tracing
out trajectories, registering the old knowledge, and projecting
new directions for inquiry. In the context of Ahab's hunt for
the white whale, the scene serves an important narrative function:
that is, to explain to the reader just how one experienced fisher-
man, using detailed geographical and historical knowledge, could
indeed locate a single whale in so vast a space as the world's
oceans. But just as Ahab uses his pencil to fill in "spaces that
before were blank," the "shifting gleams and shadows of lines"
mark the blank spaces of Ahab himself, who in a much more figurative sense represents a territory to be explored, to be mapped,
and to be known. At this moment in the novel, the immense
magnitude of the world-system and the enigma of the tragic hero
coincide in an explicitly cartographic image. In order to make
sense of this world, at both the macroscopic level of the terraqueous globe and the microscopic level of the individual subject,
Melville employs a literary technique that is itself fundamentally
a form of mapping. In examining both the real places of the geographical globe and the imaginary places of his own fictional universe, Melville's literary cartography discloses the *real-and-imagined*
spaces of the world, as Edward Soja (1996) has called them.

The act of writing itself might be considered a form of mapping or a cartographic activity. Like the mapmaker, the writer
must survey territory, determining which features of a given
landscape to include, to emphasize, or to diminish; for example,
some shadings may need to be darker than others, some lines
bolder, and so on. The writer must establish the scale and the
shape, no less of the narrative than of the places in it. The literary
cartographer, even one who operates in such non-realistic modes
as myth or fantasy, must determine the degree to which a given
representation of a place refers to any "real" place in the geographical world. In this chapter, I will discuss the ways in which
writers function as mapmakers, and I will point to certain aspects
of the theory of literature as literary cartography.

First, I will look at the general notion of literary cartography, whereby the creative writer or the writer of narrative engages in an activity quite similar to mapmaking. It is true that this is metaphorical, as the map becomes a figure for the linguistic and imaginative activity of writing, but it is also true that there are narrative maps. That is to say, a map is not only a geometrical figure like a grid, a visual archive like a table, or even a work of graphic art like a painting; a map may also constitute itself in words. There is an almost simultaneous figurative and literal aspect of literary cartography, and the writer engaged in such a project need not always be self-consciously mapping. Sometimes the very act of telling a story is also a process of producing a map. And this operates in both directions, of course: storytelling involves mapping, but a map also tells a story, and the inter-relations between space and writing tend to generate new places and new narratives. As Peter Turchi has put it in *Maps of the Imagination: The Writer as Cartographer*, "To ask for a map is to say, 'Tell me a story'" (2004: 11).

After my initial and general discussion of literary cartography, I will explore the theory of the writer as mapmaker through various theories of narrative, including a discussion of genre, and especially Russian critic Mikhail Bakhtin's influential concept of the *chronotope*, a "time-space" represented and organized by the novelistic genres Bakhtin analyses. Then, by looking briefly at philologist Erich Auerbach's influential argument concerning the "representation of reality in Western literature," as his monumental 1946 study *Mimesis* is subtitled, I argue that the relationship between the individual author in the world that the literary work purports to represent is fundamentally spatial, as well as temporal or historical, and that the distinction among various modes of literary representation is closely tied to the different ways of seeing and representing these real and imagined spaces. The Hungarian literary theorist Georg Lukács (1885–1971), in his delineation of the distinctions between epic and novel forms, draws attention to the relationship between narrative and mapping in intriguing ways. All three of these influential critics understand literary forms or genres as approaches to understanding the world, that is, of making sense of or giving form to the world. For each theorist, narrative form is thus tied to a cartographic project. Then, discussing the characterization of the ancient world whose dominant narrative form is the epic, I will argue alongside these other critics that the advent of modernity as discussed in Chapter 1, with the rise of linear perspective, of abstract or mathematical space, and of the capitalist mode of production, called for new ways of mapping such spaces in literature. Not surprisingly, the new form of literary cartography is the modern novel itself. In Lukács's view, for example, the novel is a response to a condition of "transcendental homelessness" (1971: 121), in which the individual or collective subject must now create a cosmos in order to make his own existence intelligible and meaningful.

Lukács's conception of "transcendental homelessness" is suggestive of the existential condition later described by twentieth-century philosophers Martin Heidegger and Jean-Paul Sartre. In Heidegger's view, the experience of being in the world is occasioned by an intense anxiety and a sense of the uncanny, which Sigmund Freud had also analysed. The word *uncanny* in German (*unheimlich*) actually suggests an "unhomeliness," and Heidegger writes that the feeling of anxiety (or, in German, *angst*) is fundamentally a sense of not being "at home" in the world. In part, the existentialist philosophy of Sartre derives from his understanding of Heidegger's notion of being in the world, but unlike Heidegger Sartre does not seek to restore mankind to some sort of primordial, more holistic sense of place. Rather, Sartre's theory, while acknowledging the real anguish that accompanies a person's sense of being lost, demands that individuals develop projects by which to give our lives meaning, or to put it in a vernacular more suited to space and spatial relations, to re-establish our sense of place in the world. A crucial element in the formation of such projects is the faculty of the imagination itself, which make Sartre's philosophy rather suggestive of literary cartography as well.

Finally, I will examine Fredric Jameson's influential conception of cognitive mapping, which partly derives in meaningful ways from these other literary critics and philosophers. Jameson's notion offers a model of a literary cartography which moves beyond the existentialist project and becomes a means by which a writer can supersede the individual's sense of place or placeless-ness by projecting a supra-individual image of the world-system itself. With an aesthetic of cognitive mapping, Jameson arrives at a conception for understanding the world and our place in the world, but he also provides a tool by which the world may be changed or other worlds imagined. Indeed, a sort of cognitive mapping undergirds the project of literary representation itself, whether conceived in terms of allegory or limited to supposedly realistic writing. The writer who sets out to map the world, to trace lines and shadows upon the blank spaces of the page, also makes possible other worlds.

THE WRITER AS MAPMAKER

In his meticulous and thorough reading of Herodotus' *Histories*, the ancient Greek text written in the fifth century BCE and widely considered the first work of history in Western civilization, the French historian François Hartog has observed that narrative is the result of both the geographical project of the *surveyor* and the work of a **rhapsode**, a term used in its technical or etymological sense of a "weaver," as one who thus weaves disparate parts into a whole. For Hartog, the narrator of these texts becomes, by turns but also simultaneously, a surveyor of spaces, a rhapsode who sews these spaces into a new unity, and a bard who ultimately "invents" the world so surveyed and stitched together. Referring to the *oikoumene*, the ancient Greek word for "world," Hartog writes:

> The narrator is thus a surveyor and, in a number of senses, a rhapsode, but he is also a bard, in that the inventory of the *oikoumene* cannot fail to be an invention of the world, if only by reason of the use of the space of language, for correlations exist between "the order of the discourse" and the order of the world. ... As [Herodotus] produced his inventory of distant peoples and border territories, did he not invent the *oikoumene* and set the human world in order? The space of the narrative purports to be a representation of the world and he, the rhapsode, is the one who *eidea semainei*, who

indicates the forms, who makes things seen, who reveals; he is the one who knows.

(Hartog 1988: 354–55)

Narrative, according to this view, is a form of world-making, at least as much as it is a mode of world-representing, which in the end may come to the same thing. As narrators or writers survey the territory they wish to describe, they weave together disparate elements in order to produce the narrative, and these elements may include scraps of other narratives, descriptions of people or places, images derived from first-hand observation as well as from secondary reports, legends, myths, and inventions of the imagination. In producing this patchwork representation of a world (that is, the narrative itself), the narrator also invents or discovers the world presented in the narrative. For readers, this narrative makes possible an image of the world, much like that of a map, and the literary cartography present in one narrative can become a part of future surveys, rhapsodies, and narratives, or of future narrative maps.

Literary cartography, as I am using this term, need not be limited to narrative works. It is certainly true that iconographic poetry or non-narrative description could appear to be all the more map-like, insofar as they already appear to be straightforward representations of space, whether in the forms of various spatial arrangements of lines on a page or of depictions of the geographical space exterior to literature. Narrative, on the contrary, would seem more closely tied to time, as *narrative* by definition retains a powerfully temporal aspect. That is, narrative entails the temporality of the plot—a beginning, middle, and end—whereas, arguably, a short poem maintains "a spatial form" in which all parts are present at once (see Frank 1991: 18). However, as more critics have recognized in recent decades, narrative is also spatial, and the beginnings, middles, and ends of a given story may refer as much to sites or locations in a particular spatial organization as to moments in time in a temporal one. Indeed, the very idea of *plot* is also spatial, since a plot is also a plan, which is to say, a map. Plotting or emplotment can already be understood as establishing a setting, setting a course, or marking features of an imaginative landscape. Moreover, as Jameson has put it, if narrative is the "central function or *instance* of the human mind" (1981: 13), then narrative is crucial to the ways that humans understand or make sense of their world, and it is a spatiotemporal world, to be sure. The literary cartography produced by works of literature are themselves means of giving form to the world. Non-narrative literature may also engage in a sort of mapping project, then, but the literary cartography produced through narrative may have more salient or meaningful effects.

Turchi's *Maps of the Imagination*, which deals with a variety of literary forms, explores in some detail the idea of a writer as mapmaker. It is not a work of criticism or theory exactly, although it certainly covers much of the same territory. Rather, Turchi's somewhat impressionistic or associative exploration is intended as a guide for writers and readers. A professor of creative writing, Turchi wishes to demonstrate how literary and cartographic practices overlap, infuse one another, and ultimately blend together to form what I refer to as literary cartography. Turchi is not shy about admitting that his usage is metaphorical, but he insists that the map is itself a kind of metaphor; that is, the figured place on a map is not the "real" place. In showing how the creative writer's work is a form of mapmaking, Turchi identifies five general categories or processes: "selection and omission; conventions (adherence to and departure from); inclusion and order; shape, or matters of form; and the balance of intuition and intention" (2004: 25). Of these, I wish to focus on the first, selection and omission, but these other aspects are implied throughout in the consideration of literary cartography.

To begin with, the writer, not unlike the cartographer, must determine what elements to include in the story or map. This question already implies others, such as the following: What are the function of this story or map? What do I want the reader to get out of it? What counts as a place (or event, character, or theme) worth marking? What can safely be left out?

The interrelations between space and literature, mapping and writing, description and narration, are as complex and numerous as they are interesting. In order to know a place, one maps it, but one also reads it and narrates it. In *Space and Place: The Perspective of Experience*, the geographer Yi-Fu Tuan has noted that a given portion of space becomes a "place" once it occasions a pause, a resting of the eyes that, however brief, makes it into a subject for storytelling. As one's eyes rest upon something long enough to distinguish it as a concrete presence within an undifferentiated sweep of scenery, it takes on *meanings*, traditionally the bailiwick of "literary art" (Tuan 1977: 161–62). Conversely, a literary work becomes infused with the places that it explores, and that make it what it is. Often, the story and the place are inextricably bound together.

In Italo Calvino's postmodern novel *Invisible Cities*, the narrator, Marco Polo, describes places he has seen to the Kublai Khan. The narrator expresses some mild frustration at the overlapping of geography and storytelling, when he struggles to make known a place, which cannot simply be described in strictly spatial or geographical terms, since what makes a *place* noteworthy is often the narratives that give it meaning. As he puts it:

In vain, great-hearted Kublai, shall I attempt to describe Zaira, city of high bastions. I could tell you how many steps make up the streets rising like stairways, and the degree of the arcades' curves, and what kind of zinc scales cover the roofs; but I already know this would be the same as telling you nothing. The city does not consist of this, but of relationships between the measurements of its space and the events of its past: the height of a lamppost and the distance from the ground of a hanged usurper's swaying feet; the line strung from the lamppost to the railing opposite and the festoons that decorate the course of the queen's nuptial procession; the height of that railing and the leap of the adulterer who climbed over it at dawn; the tilt of a guttering and a cat's progress along it as he slips into the same window; the firing range of a gunboat which has suddenly appeared beyond the cape and the bomb that destroys the guttering; the rips in the fish net and the three old men seated on the dock mending nets and telling each other for the hundredth time the story of the gunboat of the usurper, who some say was the queen's illegitimate son, abandoned in his swaddling clothes there on the dock.

> As this wave from memories flows in, the city soaks it up like a sponge and expands. A description of Zaira as it is today should contain all Zaira's past. The city, however, does not tell its past, but contains it like the lines of a hand, written in the corners of the streets, the gratings of the windows, the banisters of the steps, the antennae of the lightning rods, the poles of the flags, every segment marked in turn with scratches, indentations, scrolls.
>
> (1974: 10–11)

Here the most minute details of a particular place, such as the height of a banister, are crucial to an entire history, which includes elements of forbidden love, political intrigue, warfare and folklore, and perhaps much more. As Calvino's example makes clear, space and storytelling thus merge, and then emerge, as part of a broader literary geography, which in turn becomes the ground for a writer's own literary cartography, and hence the subject of a spatially orientated literary criticism. Calvino's point, that one cannot describe a place without also narrating the stories embedded in the site, makes explicit something that is arguably implicit in all writings, which must come to terms with the spatiotemporality of narrative.

In contrast to Calvino's position, perhaps, James Joyce famously stated in an interview that, in *Ulysses*, "I want to give a picture of Dublin so complete that if the city one day suddenly disappeared from the earth, it could be reconstructed out of my book" (Budgen 1989: 69). *Ulysses* is imagined as a narrative map, even a blueprint, of the city of Dublin itself. Of course, Joyce's stated desire here reflects the degree to which a writer's cartographic project is ultimately impossible, doomed to failure in advance, but also capable of failing in interesting ways. The spaces represented in the novel cannot be the same as the "real" space, what Barbara Piatti calls **geospace** in contrast to the imagined space in literary texts (see Piatti 2008: 22–23), of a city or country. But, as I will discuss in the next chapter, that does not stop true fans from trying to bring the "real" places of a city directly into line with the "imaginary" world they explored in their readings. For instance, even the prodigiously learned philosopher and semiotician Umberto Eco (1932–) once admitted that "we all know that there are people who go looking for Sherlock Holmes's house in Baker Street, and I happen to be one of those who has gone looking for the house in Eccles Street in Dublin where Leopold Bloom is supposed to have lived" (Eco 1994: 84). The imaginary space of the novel and the real, geospace of Dublin are clearly connected, but they do not coincide exactly, and Joyce's comment must be taken to reflect an ironic ambition, no less meaningful for being ironic.

As much as *Ulysses* might have to offer to the reader who wishes to know Dublin as it actually is, Joyce's novel is hardly a manual or guidebook for city-planners. The mapping project of narrative is necessarily incomplete, provisional, and tentative. And that is almost certainly a good thing. For example, the French novelist Georges Perec (1936–1982), in his remarkably ambitious and postmodern experiment called *Attempt at Exhausting a Place in Paris* (2010, originally published in 1974), endeavoured to "see what happens when nothing happens" by spending three days monitoring a single location in Paris and recording everything he saw. As the literary critic Bertrand Westphal observed of Perec's experiment, it would have remained incomplete even if he had "camped out in the heart of the Sahara," but "Perec instead chose to engage with the bustling Place Saint-Sulpice," a busy urban locale, where far more was going on than could possibly be noticed, much less narrated or described. As Westphal put it, "Although he was confined to one location at a specific time, the project was actually boundless" (Westphal 2011: 150). Indeed, merely enumerating the buses that pulled up at the bus stop would quickly become tedious, not to mention describing other vehicles, pedestrian passers-by, their clothing and overall appearance, the dogs or birds, and so on. Moreover, beyond the visual archive, Perec needed to bring the other senses into play, by describing, for example, the feel of the midday sun, the smell of diesel fumes, and the sounds of children crying. Ironically, perhaps, all this attention to detail and almost indiscriminate recording of information ultimately leads to a failure, not only to "exhaust the place" entirely (which, in any case, would be impossible), but also to register the uniqueness of the place chosen. After all, when one starts focusing on such apparently insignificant details as the passing-by of the Number 86 bus, what difference does it make that the author is at Place Saint-Sulpice in Paris, as opposed to some other town in France, or elsewhere in Europe or even the world? A Number 86 bus might as well be driving past one's coffee shop in Durham, North Carolina. Hence, the literary cartography of Place Saint-Sulpice is not well served by this exhausting method.

The writer, then, must select the particulars of a given place or story that will allow for the narrative map to be meaningful. This is equally true for an actual mapmaker, who must determine the function of the map and its intended "meanings" for a map-reader prior to setting down the elements on paper. Will this map be used only by motorists, as with most roadmaps? If pedestrians will not be using the map, then perhaps footpaths may be omitted. Many coastal charts must include information that makes little sense in other contexts; for example, the depth of water at low tide is an essential bit of information for navigating beaches and estuaries, but it is probably irrelevant to those compiling urban street-maps. The height of buildings or radio towers matters little to taxi drivers, but such information may be of crucial importance to helicopter pilots. Similarly, a story lacking essential elements or, in contrast, containing too many inessential ones, will fail to deliver the proper "place" to its readers. And, as with Hartog's discussion of the writer as surveyor, rhapsode, and bard, the author of a narrative produces the world through the narrative, thereby rendering it meaningful. A failure in this enterprise can be more serious than a mere inaccurate picture, as all maps are technically inaccurate or incomplete; the failure is to render one "lost" in space.

GENRE AND THE LITERARY CHRONOTOPE

By determining the elements of a story or map, by choosing which elements will be prominent and which can remain in the background, and by arranging the elements in a way best suited to the intended effects that writer or cartographer wishes the work to have upon the reader, the author is also determining what *kind* of narrative or map this will be. Hence, the literary cartography necessarily involves a question of genre. Following John Frow's excellent study of *Genre* (2006), I might suggest that genre is itself a sort of map, since the generic parameters help to establish the projected "world" of the story.

Frow's overall definition of *genre* demonstrates the degree to which genre is similar to, or perhaps part of, mapping. Genres, like maps, are essential in organizing knowledge in such a way as to make things meaningful, and both the generic frame and the map, as noted earlier, project a *world*, which Frow understands as a "relatively bounded and schematic domain of meanings, values, and affects" (85–86); he continues:

> Genre, we might say, is a set of conventional and highly organized constraints on the production and interpretation of meaning. In using the word "constraint" I don't mean to say that genre is simply a restriction. Rather, its structuring effects are productive of meaning; they shape and guide, in the way that a builder's form gives shape to the pour of concrete, or a sculptor's mould shapes and gives structure to its materials. Generic structure both enables and restricts meaning, and is a basic condition for meaning to take place. I take it that genre theory is, or should be, about the ways in which different structures of meaning and truth are produced in and by the various kinds of writing, talking, painting, filming, and acting by which the universe of discourse is structured. That is why genre matters: it is central to human meaning-making and to the social struggle over meanings. No speaking or writing or any other symbolically organized action takes place other than through the shapings of generic codes, where "shaping" means both "shaping by" and "shaping of": acts and structures work upon and modify each other.
>
> (Frow 2006: 10)

Similarly, the map both uses genre and is a sort of genre, as the map also shapes the different bits of data into a meaningful ensemble to be interpreted and understood; and the map, like the genre, both structures this world and is a structure within a world.

Moreover, as rapidly becomes clear, the genres can be understood in relation to their organization of space and time, among the other elements of a narrative. To take but one example, the Gothic romance calls to mind a certain kind of landscape, whose buildings maintain a distinct architectural style. The ways in which this or that character moves within, negotiates, or becomes immured to the spaces of a Gothic romance will be quite different from the manner in which such activities occur in an allegorical epic poem or a picaresque satire. As Jameson has noted, "Genres are essentially literary *institutions*, or social contracts between a writer and a specific public, whose function is to specify the proper use of a cultural artifact" (1981: 106). In this case also, we might liken genre to a guidebook, whereby the writer, in utilizing or specifying the recognizable elements of a given genre, provides the reader a kind of "You Are Here," with identifiable points of reference that can enable the reader to reach the desired destination. The author, like the cartographer, employs conventional techniques or strategies in trying to prevent the reader of the text or map from getting lost. As Jameson concludes, without reference to the implicit spatiality of the project, "No small part of the art of writing, indeed, is absorbed by this (impossible) attempt to design a foolproof mechanism for the automatic exclusion of undesirable responses to a given literary utterance" (1981: 206–7).

Mikhail Bakhtin (1895–1975), a Russian literary critic and philosopher of language, coined the term *chronotope*, which literally suggests "time-space," in order to make clearer sense of the relations between historical time and geographical space in literature. Bakhtin also imagines the idea of the chronotope as a way of understanding the "generic techniques that have been devised for reflecting and artistically processing" aspects of time and space (Bakhtin 1981: 84). Of crucial importance to Bakhtin is the fact that space and time are inextricably bound together, and he considers the chronotope as "a formally constitutive category of literature" (1981: 84). Bakhtin's chronotope is another tool both for comprehending and producing literary cartography, as the chronotope brings space, time, and genre together in a conceptually integrated way.

Bakhtin does not provide a definitive or detailed treatment of the theory of the literary chronotope, but rather he allows its terminological flexibility to cover a number of related notions. Hence, at times the chronotope primarily appears to be defined by its respective genre, such as the chronotope of the ancient Greek romance, while in other moments it seems to refer to a particular spatiotemporal figure within a work or genre, such as "the road" as distinctive chronotope. Yet for all usages, Bakhtin emphasizes the degree to which a narrative projects a recognizable time-space that can then inform the historical poetics he attempts to elaborate. As Bakhtin states:

> In the literary artistic chronotope, spatial and temporal indicators are fused into one carefully thought-out, concrete whole. Time, as it were, thickens, takes on flesh, becomes artistically visible; likewise, space becomes charged and responsive to the movements of time, plot and history. This intersection of axes and fusion of indicators characterizes the artistic chronotope.
>
> (1981: 84)

To summarize briefly, Bakhtin's discussion of the chronotope in the development of narrative forms or genres leads from the ancient Greek romance with its "adventure chronotope" and abstract space, through the ancient Roman novels of Apuleius and Petronius where "space becomes more concrete and saturated with a time that is more substantial" (1981: 120), to ancient biography and autobiography whose focus on the time and space of the individual would "exercise enormous influence ... on the development of the novel" (146). In moving from "the ancient forms of the novel," as he calls them, to the "folk-loric chronotope, the chivalric romance, and the *carnivalesque* fiction of François Rabelais, Bakhtin identifies a movement in narrative forms similar to that identified by Georg Lukács in *The Theory of the Novel* (first published 1916), but Bakhtin does not view the shifting chronotopes or narrative forms as a degra-dation of some earlier unity or integrated totality. Rather, he finds that the proliferation of various voices and the historical "inversions" of myth and history offer moments of democratic or revolutionary potential. For both Lukács and Bakhtin, but with different valences attached to their arguments, the parodic

Don Quixote (1605–1615) serves as a turning point. But Bakhtin, who had written a lengthy study on *Rabelais and His World* (1984), pays greater attention to "the Rabelaisian chronotope," which presents a "new picture of the world ... polemically opposed to the medieval world" (171). Finally, Bakhtin examines the "idyllic chronotope" and its development in the eighteenth and nineteenth centuries.

For this attenuated rehearsal of Bakhtin's essay, "Forms of Time and of the Chronotope in the Novel: Notes Toward a Historical Poetics" (first published 1937–1938), I have not highlighted the ways in which the concept of the chronotope relates to literary cartography or narrative mapping, but it is clear that the conception already elevates space to a level equal to (and, in fact, inseparable from) time in the study of narratives, something that puts Bakhtin slightly ahead of the spatial turn in literary studies.

In his "concluding remarks," added some 35 years after the original essay, Bakhtin argues that chronotopes are "the organizing centres for the fundamental narrative events of the novel. The chronotope is the place where the knots of the narrative are tied and untied. It can be said without qualification that to them belongs the meaning that shapes narrative" (1981: 250). As this bold characterization makes clear, the chronotope is a critical element of any literary cartography, for it is through the use of and reference to particular chronotopes that the meaning of the narrative, the shape of the world, is established. However, here it is also certain that the individual writer or mapmaker is not simply making choices, selections or omissions, but is participating (perhaps even unwittingly) in larger historical and cultural processes by which these moments and places gain greater significance. As Bakhtin concedes, "The represented world, however realistic and truthful, can never be chronotopically identical with the real world it represents, where the author and creator of the literary work is found" (256). These broader and more complex relations among the world, the text, and the literary cartographer point to the supra-individual or historical forms discussed in Lukács's theory of the novel.

FORM AND THE REPRESENTATION OF REALITY

In *The Formal Method of Literary Scholarship*, a work frequently attributed to Bakhtin but perhaps written collectively by members of the "Bakhtin Circle," Pavel Medvedev writes that for the novelist "the reality of the genre is the social reality of its realization in the process of artistic intercourse," which is to say that the writer organizes "life as he sees it onto the plane of the work." Thus, "genre is the aggregate of the means of collective orientation in reality," and "this orientation is capable of mastering new aspects of reality" (Bakhtin/Medvedev 1978: 135). This conception of genre is very similar to what I am calling literary cartography, particularly where "aspects of reality" are understood to include those of social space. The representation of reality, a goal of both narratives and maps, is thus tied to genre, which Medvedev also calls "the aggregate of the means for seeing and conceptualizing reality" (137).

The phrase "representation of reality" might be used to describe the goals of both literature and cartography, provided it is understood that both fields only represent reality through figurative means. If various genres, such as the epic or the novel, represent reality in particular, identifiable, and distinctive ways, then one might say that literary cartography is determined, at least in part, by narrative form.

Erich Auerbach (1892–1957), another major early twentieth-century critic who was a contemporary of Bakhtin and Lukács and who addressed some of the same literary historical issues, is best known for his magisterial study, *Mimesis: The Representation of Reality in Western Literature* (1953; first published 1946). Even earlier, in a book on Dante, Auerbach had made the astonishing claim that, despite being the author of the "divine" *Commedia*, Dante was "the poet of the earthly world" (2001; first published in 1929). Although translated into English as "secular," which is already a potential scandalous reading of what seemed a very religious work, Auerbach's original German word, *irdische*, suggests not only worldly or secular, but earthy or "of the earth." And, although most scholars of twentieth-century criticism would not associate Auerbach with taking part in the spatial turn in literary studies, his philological studies are always grounded in a sense of the connection to the spaces and places of an author's experience. What is more, Auerbach's influence is apparent in the works of a number of later spatially oriented critics, especially Edward Said and Fredric Jameson.

In *Mimesis*, Auerbach offers a different view of the representational processes of the epic from that of either Bakhtin or Lukács, and the famous contrast between the styles of Homer's *Odyssey* and the Old Testament book of Genesis with which he opens his study is instructive. Auerbach examines these two well known, ancient texts and observes how differently each approaches the presentation of its scene. He focuses on the section of Book XIX of the *Odyssey* where the nurse Eurycleia discovers Odysseus' scar while bathing his leg, thus identifying him and revealing that the King has at last returned home to Ithaca. At precisely that point in the narrative, Homer takes the reader on a lengthy excursus that explains the origin of the scar, which Odysseus had received from a wound incurred while hunting wild boars as a youth. That is, at a moment filled with suspense and excitement concerning the momentous events in the present, Homer provides a flashback intended to fill in the gaps in the reader's knowledge and to provide detailed substance for what otherwise might have been blank spaces. In contrast to this, Auerbach examines the narration of the scene in Genesis where God calls Abraham to sacrifice his son Isaac. In that scene, almost no context is given, and there is certainly no indication of time or place. If God is speaking to Abraham, where is he? God calls out to him, and Abraham answers "I am here," but the actual location does not matter to the author of Genesis. That is, unlike in the *Odyssey*, the Genesis author is content to leave much in the background or completely unknown, while focusing on only those elements deemed essential to the purpose of the narrative. As Auerbach understands it, these differences underlie two rather distinct approaches to **mimesis** or the representation of reality itself.

To put the matter differently, it is not merely a case of the author's selectivity in choosing to produce this as opposed to that kind of map. Rather, as Auerbach analyses them, these are two quite different ways of imagining literary cartography in general.

In one case, the aim is to present something like a complete "worldly" world within the narrative, filling in all the blanks, whereas the other takes the worldly elements to be irrelevant, placing an otherworldly or mystical experience in a far more prominent position. As Auerbach says:

> It would be difficult, then, to imagine styles more contrasted than those of these two equally ancient and equally epic texts. On the one hand, externalized, uniformly illuminated phenomena, at a definite time and in a definite place, connected together without lacunae in a perpetual foreground; thoughts and feeling completely expressed; events taking place in leisurely fashion and with very little of suspense. On the other hand, the externalization of only so much of the phenomena as is necessary for the purpose of the narrative, all else left in obscurity; the decisive points of the narrative alone are emphasized, what lies between is non-existent; time and place are undefined and call for interpretation; thoughts and feeling remain unexpressed, are only suggested by the silence and the fragmentary speeches; the whole, permeated with the most unrelieved suspense and directed toward a single goal (and to that extent far more of a unity), remains mysterious and "fraught with background."
>
> (Auerbach 1953: 11–12)

Following Auerbach, we could say that these differing styles produce different maps. Neither map could be wholly comprehensive, of course, and Homer does leave much out of the mythic history of Odysseus, but within the narrative of the epic, Homer's "map" strives to lay out the geographical knowledge in a more or less uniform way; the Genesis "map," in contrast, obscures certain aspects and emphasizes others, which requires the map-reader to read "between the lines" of the figured spaces. Auerbach concludes:

> The two styles, in their opposition, represent basic types: on the one hand fully externalized description, uniform illumination, uninterrupted connection, free expression, all events in the foreground, displaying unmistakable meanings, few elements of historical development and of psychological perspective; on the other hand, certain

parts brought into high relief, others left obscure, abruptness, suggestive influence of the unexpressed, "background" quality, multiplicity of meanings and the need for interpretation, universal-historical claims, development of the concept of the historically becoming, and pre-occupation with the problematic.

(1953: 23)

Auerbach's study begins with these two ancient texts, and then touches on various works all the way up to the near present, finishing with an analysis of Virginia Woolf's *To the Lighthouse* (first published 1927). He thus takes these two styles as competing models for how Western literature will represent reality in general, over thousands of years. As a far-ranging study of a sort of European realism, questioning "to what degree and in what manner realistic subjects were treated seriously, problematically, or tragically" (1953: 556), Auerbach's *Mimesis* establishes a way of seeing how a kind of literary cartography develops and is deployed.

Another key theorist of narrative, working roughly in the same era as Bakhtin and Auerbach, is the Hungarian philosopher and literary critic Georg Lukács (1885–1971). In his magnificent early study, *The Theory of the Novel* (1971; first published in 1920), Lukács distinguishes between the age of the epic and that of the novel, arguing from a Hegelian standpoint that the modern world, in which the novel is the representative literary form, is typified by a fragmentation and open-endedness. Lukács begins with a rather poetic, and somewhat cartographic, depiction of the age of the epic. "Happy are those ages when the starry sky is a map of all possible paths—ages whose paths are illuminated by the light of the stars. Everything in such ages is new and yet familiar, full of adventure and yet their own. The world is wide and yet it is like a home" (1971: 29).

Lukács maintains that "the epic gives form to a totality of life that is rounded from within; the novel seeks, by giving form, to uncover and construct the concealed totality of life" (60). For Lukács, the world of the epic is that of an integrated or closed (in the sense of complete) totality, in which both character and narrative form are relatively static. "Nestor is old just as

Helen is beautiful or Agamemnon mighty" (121), and Lukács finds that "the way Homer's epics begin in the middle and do not finish at the end is a reflection of the epic mentality's total indifference to any form of architectural construction" (67). After all, in Lukács's view, since the epic world is already an integrated totality, the narrative form need not project or organize the world's disparate elements into a totality. Bakhtin, in an early essay on the distinction, would seem to agree: "the epic past is absolute and complete. It is as closed as a circle; inside it everything is finished, already over. There is no place in the epic world for any openendedness, indecision, indeterminacy" (Bakhtin 1981: 16).

From this perspective, the advent of the age of the novel coincides with the fragmentation of this imagined, ancient coherence or totality. Whereas the epic could reflect the integrated civilization of the ancient Greeks, the novel will have as its vocation the projection of an imaginary, perhaps provisional and contingent, totality, since there is no longer one that we can simply assume. Lukács argues that "[t]he novel is the epic of an age in which the extensive totality of life is no longer directly given, in which the immanence of meaning in life has become a problem, yet which still thinks in terms of totality" (Lukács 1971: 56), a claim that he also repeats more rhetorically in the statement that "[t]he novel is the epic of a world that has been abandoned by God" (88).

As we have already seen, Lukács's image of the unified totality of the ancients is both Romantic, inasmuch as it posits a lost organic wholeness for which we moderns yearn in vain, and largely erroneous, since, as Hartog and others have discovered, the ancient world also required the surveying of spaces, knitting these spaces together, and projecting a world. Yet Lukács's evocative notion of the novel form as an expression of "transcendental homelessness" (1971: 41) is of direct relevance to much of the more directly spatial discourse in twentieth-century philosophy and literary theory. As I will discuss in the following sections, this sense of "homelessness" occasions the need for a kind of mapping, and the artistic forms associated with literary cartography undoubtedly derive their force and their desirability from the general unease with respect to our sense of place, what Lukács would have likened to a loss of a sense of totality; he observes, "[a]rt, the visionary reality of the world made to our measure, has thus become independent: it is no longer a copy, for all the models have gone; it is a created totality, for the natural unity of the metaphysical spheres has been destroyed forever" (37). Although it appears almost nostalgic in the early Lukács, perhaps against his will, the representation of reality in a world abandoned by God makes possible the more positive cartographic projects to be found later in Sartre or Jameson.

ANXIETY AND A SENSE OF PLACE

Although it derives from a slightly different philosophical tradition and is used to serve different ends, Lukács's evocative conception of "transcendental homelessness" is a precursor to the notion of existential *angst* that would become a powerful influence on literary and popular culture, especially in the post-Second World War period. Existentialism is most closely associated with the early writings of the German philosopher Martin Heidegger (1889–1976), especially his 1927 treatise *Being and Time* (translation 1962) and the French philosopher, critic, novelist, and playwright Jean-Paul Sartre (1905–1980), who did much to popularize the term itself in his writing, including his 1947 essay *Existentialism is a Humanism* (translation 2007). Existentialism is not a formal school of philosophy, of course, and many of its apparent precepts and ideas may be found in the works of creative writers, philosophers, psychologists, sociologists, and historians, many of whom would shun the label *existentialist*. Yet, the basic terms from existentialist discourse, like much of Freudian psychoanalysis or Marxist political theory, have entered into the vocabulary and thinking of everyday life. Also, I argue, the fundamental sense of placelessness and bewilderment that is now associated with the postmodern condition or with postindustrial society is akin to that pervasive feeling of anxiety analysed by Heidegger and Sartre, among others.

The German word *Angst*, translated variously as and used interchangeably with *anxiety*, *dread*, or *anguish* (and sometimes left untranslated, as the term in its existentialist sense has moved into English), designates a key concept in existentialism. In Sartre's view, anxiety is the necessary predicate of the basic, existential condition in which "existence precedes essence," as that phrase was deployed by Sartre in *Being and Nothingness*, among other works. Sartre draws upon Heidegger's statement in *Being and Time* that "The 'essence' of Dasein lies in its existence" (Heidegger 1962: 67), where "Dasein" represents one's being in the world itself; that is, Sartre maintains, the inescapable characteristic of being-in-the-world is simply that it exists. In existence, one is situated in a world and cannot otherwise be; one cannot seek external, transcendent, or eternal grounds for justifying one's own existence or for finding some essence or meaning apart from the world. Sartre concludes from this that one must have the freedom to create one's own meaningful existence, establishing a sense of place and purpose in the world, via a project in which the individual subject orchestrates the elements or aspects of life in some meaningful way.

Referring to this as the "first principle of existentialism," Sartre explains his understanding of the phrase:

> What do we mean here by "existence precedes essence"? We mean that man first exists: he materializes in the world, encounters himself, and only afterwards defines himself. If man as existentialists conceive of him cannot be defined, it is because to begin with he is nothing. He will not be anything until later, and then he will be what he makes of himself.
>
> (2007: 22)

Such freedom is deduced from a general uneasiness, a mood that Sartre dramatizes as "nausea" in the 1938 novel of that name, and which is the bodily manifestation of anguish, fear, or anxiety. In Sartre's assessment, the anxiety one feels derives from the fact that "man is condemned to be free: condemned, because he did not create himself, yet nonetheless free, because once cast into the world, he is responsible for everything he does" (2007: 29). Anxiety comes from not knowing whether one's actions are correct (or, indeed, from knowing that *no* action is essentially right or wrong), thereby acknowledging, albeit negatively, that one must have the freedom to choose the right or wrong path. Hence, the very feeling of anxiety is a visceral human acknowledgement of inescapable freedom.

But if freedom is the source of existential anxiety, then freedom for Sartre is also the means by which it can be overcome. Anxiety, born alongside the freedom to act, inevitably carries with it a pervasive sense of alienation. That is, one experiences a sensation of the *uncanny*, a generalized discomfort that may not always be easily described, the sort of nameless dread that the Danish philosopher Søren Kierkegaard (1813–1855) discusses in his 1843 treatise *Fear and Trembling*, and one which continues to be modelled by filmmakers working in the genre of horror. In *Being and Time*, Heidegger had already asserted that anxiety is always tied to the uncanny, a term that in German retains its sense of the unfamiliar, since *unheimlich* suggests "un-homely": "In anxiety one feels 'uncanny' [*unheimlich*]. Here the peculiar indefiniteness of that which Dasein finds itself alongside in anxiety, comes proximally to expression: the 'nothing and nowhere.' But here 'uncanniness' also means 'not-being-at-home' [*das Nicht-zuhause-sein*]" (1962: 233; bracketed terms in original). The world in which we are always situated is not of our own making, but our very essence (that is, existence itself) requires us to shape our world. The human condition is, as we saw earlier, fundamentally one of "not being at home," which calls to mind Lukács's assessment of modernity as a state of "transcendental homelessness." But this then invites a discussion of the ways in which the anxiety-ridden person engages with the defamiliarized or uncanny space in which she finds herself.

Sartre's answer is that we create meaning or give shape to our existence through our projects. In the anxiety that causes one to feel disoriented or lost, one has the freedom to project a kind of schematic representation of the world and one's place in it that becomes a way of making sense of things. The project then becomes a kind of figurative cartography, through which it is possible to overcome this disorientation, or in Heidegger's sense this "not-at-home-ness," by making sense of, or giving form to, the world. In other words, by mapping, partly a metaphor for constellating the various forces that directly and indirectly affect human life, but here with a specifically spatial valence, it may be possible to overcome this anxious, transcendental homelessness. And if the human subject does not exactly feel "at home," then at least one can develop strategies for navigating these uncanny spaces of everyday life. One's project then defines, in a rather literal way, one's existence. Sartre observes that the project one undertakes necessarily interrelates to others' projects, and that the human activity of projecting is the quintessential interaction of the subject and the world. From the existentialist concepts of the early Sartre, then, we can see the outlines of another form of literary cartography, insofar as the power of the imagination to project a meaningful ensemble which can then be used to aid in the navigation of social spaces is itself a type of mapping. Indeed, what Jameson calls "cognitive mapping" involves just such a projection and, in at least one of its senses, cognitive mapping is conceived as a way to overcome the existential alienation of modern life.

AN AESTHETIC OF COGNITIVE MAPPING

As we observed in Chapter 1, Jameson's concept of cognitive mapping has been one of the most influential, and sometimes controversial, concepts in the literary and cultural theory related to the spatial turn and to postmodernism. At the same time, however, the defining characteristics of cognitive mapping have not always been clear. Part of the reason for this is that, since introducing it in his 1984 essay "Postmodernism, or, the Cultural Logic of Late Capitalism" (later revised and published as a chapter in his 1991 book of the same title), Jameson has continuously refined the meaning of the term; and, although in more recent work he has largely stopped employing the phrase "cognitive mapping," the underlying concept continues to inform his multifaceted critique of late capitalism or globalization. Indeed, as I argue, Jameson's aesthetic of cognitive mapping is central to his lifelong project of theorizing the relations between literary forms and social formations, and cognitive mapping itself is a significant model for the project of literary cartography.

Even though Jameson has remained remarkably consistent over his more than 50-year career, he has developed and used the concept of cognitive mapping in various ways. For example, *cognitive mapping* sometimes refers to an individual subject's attempt to locate his or her position within a complex social organization or spatial milieu, as in the case with a single person who is walking around in an unfamiliar city, attempting to gain a concrete sense of place in relation to various other places on a mental map. This conception reveals how cognitive mapping could be a crucial method by which to overcome the real anxiety of being lost, in the most urgent everyday sense as well as the more philosophical or existential sense. At other times, Jameson indicates a supra-individual, abstract, or "objective" production of space in the multinational, late capitalist world system, such that the project of cognitive mapping could not possibly be limited to an individual's singular perspective. The complexities of the concept are perhaps compounded by Jameson's own dialectical system of thought, in which multiple and even opposed elements are brought together under the power of some unifying or totalizing force, such as the dialectic, or capital itself. Jameson does not hesitate to embrace disparate critical theories or practices, some of which diverge significantly from the thesis he appears to put forth, only to synthesize them, incorporating these elements into his larger philosophical or critical theory. In what might be thought of as his own version of the Hegelian *Aufhebung*, a process by which concept is at once cancelled, preserved, changed, and elevated, Jameson is frequently able to cancel others' arguments, while preserving the kernel of their ideas, and dialectically advancing his own position.

Although he famously introduced the term in his 1984 essay on postmodernism, Jameson had begun to develop the concept of cognitive mapping much earlier. As I have argued in this chapter, the developments of narrative theory and the theory of the novel in the twentieth century carry with them an implicit, and sometimes explicit, conception of mapping or of spatiality. Jameson, himself a student of Auerbach's as well as a scholar and champion of the work of Lukács and other continental theorists, certainly draws upon the arguments surrounding mimesis, figuration, representation, and genre in his development of the concept of cognitive mapping. His discussions of Lukács and Sartre, as well as Walter Benjamin, Ernst Bloch, and Herbert Marcuse, in *Marxism and Form* (1971) already touch upon aspects of what will later be recognizable as cognitive mapping.

In his 1977 essay, "Class and Allegory in Contemporary Mass Culture" (which is included in his 1992 book on cinema, *Signatures of the Visible*), Jameson discusses the ways in which the *figurability* of a work of art, in this case the 1975 film *Dog Day Afternoon*, makes possible the representation of a larger, more meaningful reality, than that which the particular and localized actions of individuals depicted. Individual subjects attempt to represent the larger totality of social relations even while they are engaged in minute, rather particular, and everyday activities— in this case the botched bank robbery—but the activities of the bank robbers are ultimately less significant that the social and spatial environment in which they take place, where the viewer can discern the crumbling world of the neighbourhood grocery store, the anxious pseudo-stability of a middle-class environment, and the ominous outlines of a multinational or corporate presence that will affect all in hitherto unseen ways. Although he does not use the term in that essay, Jameson clearly had begun to formulate his notion of cognitive mapping, as he specifically acknowledges in an "afterword" (1992b: 54). In what appears to be his first explicit use of the term, in his influential 1981 study *The Political Unconscious* (1981), Jameson names the concept in his discussion of the interrelations between romance and realism. He writes that realism is "traditionally in one form or another the central model of Marxist aesthetics as a narrative discourse which unites the experience of daily life with a properly cognitive, mapping, or well-nigh 'scientific' perspective" (1981: 104). Although the words are here separated by a comma, Jameson already suggests that cognitive mapping, like literary cartography, partakes of both realism and something like romanticism, fantasy, or allegory; this is a telling point of departure given the fact that the mapping project requires figuration and mimesis in attempting to represent real and imaginary spaces.

Although I have argued in this chapter that this kind of literary cartography or mapping has been a crucial means by which we understand the world, Jameson emphasizes the historical specificity of the postmodern, or rather of the moment of multinational capitalism or globalization, in which spatial disorientation and the need for new means of representation are most pressing. In his brief survey of the postmodern condition, Jameson begins by describing the various examples of how our cultural situation in the era of globalization is radically different from, and yet also connected to, the preceding social and historical formations. Indeed, drawing in part upon Raymond Williams's discussion in *Marxism and Literature* (1977) of residual, dominant, and emergent cultural forms, Jameson recognizes that postmodernism is a "cultural dominant," but that postmodern societies also contain many of the elements of earlier ones, while simultaneously carrying the seeds of some future forms. Nevertheless, Jameson proposes that the older, realist or modernist aesthetic practices are no longer suitable or even feasible in our postmodern condition, that the worldview in which the nation-state is an organizing model can no longer offer a satisfactory map of the present global relays of power and money, and that we need to develop an aesthetic of cognitive mapping that may somehow confront the intense crisis of representation that we face in our attempts to apprehend the world system. Of course, part of the problem is also that the propensity towards fragmentariness of the postmodern condition, as elaborated by Lyotard (1984) and others, actually precludes any apprehension of a "system" as a whole. Jameson's response itself requires a somewhat modernist strategy, whereby a lost totality may be projected and represented amid the fragmentary and mobile elements of postmodern life. Literary cartography, at present, must deal with the same sort of crises.

Jameson has two main sources for this concept of cognitive mapping, one apparently more practical and the other theoretical, although theory and practice cannot long be separated. The first model of cognitive mapping is found in the American urban planner Kevin Lynch's study of urban spaces, *The Image of the City* (1960), and the second derives from the French philosopher

Louis Althusser's famous essay "Ideology and Ideological State Apparatuses" (1971). As Jameson puts it later, "cognitive mapping can now be characterized as something of a synthesis between Althusser and Kevin Lynch" (1991: 415).

Introducing such terms as *imageability* and *wayfinding* into urban studies, Lynch's *The Image of the City* focuses on the ways in which individuals or groups in cities imagine and make their way through their environments. This framework is fundamentally phenomenological; it presupposes a psychological subject who, using largely visual points of reference, can "map" the landscape and find ways to move within it. By way of illustration, Lynch compares three rather different cities (Boston, Jersey City, and Los Angeles), and he contrasts the ways that subjects see and map them. Boston, with its familiar landmarks, borders, and districts (such as the prominent John Hancock Building, the boundary-defining Charles River, or the distinctive downtown), is a city of which one can more easily form a mental diagram and through which one can move with relatively little conceptual difficulty. In contrast, Lynch's empirical research finds that Jersey City lacks the traditional markers or readily "imageable" places, and he discovered that "none of the respondents had anything like a comprehensive view of the city in which they had lived for many years. The maps were often fragmented, with large blank areas, concentrating most often on small home territories" (1960: 29). This represents a model of the alienated city, an urban space that one has difficulty mapping even while living and moving within it; it is a space characterized in part by confusion, and may be likened to that existential anxiety described in Heidegger and Sartre. Los Angeles, which would become the subject of Edward Soja's more detailed analyses in *Postmodern Geographies* (1989) and ***Thirdspace*** (1996) offers yet another alternative for Lynch. However, since that city's spaces appear to be designed for, and are in any case dominated by, automobile traffic, Los Angeles offers somewhat less of a directly lived space for its inhabitants. Of these places examined by Lynch, Boston is the most "imageable," offering the least cognitive resistance to an individual's "wayfinding" through the urban landscape.

From Lynch's analysis, Jameson proposes a working definition of cognitive mapping, which "involves the practical reconquest sense of place and the construction or reconstruction of an articulated ensemble which can be retained in memory and which the individual subject can map and remap along the moments of mobile, alternative trajectories" (1991: 51). Lynch's work was limited to the urban experience, however, and Jameson is interesting in extending this model to the national or global spaces that he takes to be more pertinent to the postmodern condition. Althusser's theory of ideology therefore provides Jameson with a model, which in turn makes possible his conceptual extension from the urban perspective of Lynch's individual, wayfinding cartographers to the global reach that Jameson's cognitive mapping will require. Althusser had defined ideology as "a representation of the imaginary relationship of individuals to their real conditions of existence" (1971: 167), and Jameson argues that this is precisely what, in theory, the individual attempting to mentally map and navigate the city is doing in practice. As I pointed out, this is quite similar to Jameson's earlier point about the novel or narrative in general in *The Political Unconscious*, where the Althusserian formulation of ideology, or rather the idea of the literary text as imagined by Pierre Macherey and Etienne Balibar (1981: 53), is suggestive of the vocation of literature itself: namely, to produce imaginary solutions to real contradictions. Hence, what Jameson's formulates as cognitive mapping is already another way of imagining literary cartography.

Although Jameson certainly believes that cognitive mapping is a strategy appropriate to the particular conditions of postmodernity or late capitalism, he provides historical examples of practices much like cognitive mapping in earlier epochs. In a section he calls a "digression on cartography," he acknowledges that the cognitive mapping in Lynch's sense of imageability and wayfinding is actually pre-cartographic, much more like itineraries than maps. (I will return to this distinction between the **itinerary** and the map in Chapter 4.) Whereas maps require a sense of overview that supersedes the perspective of a single individual, itineraries are "diagrams organized around the still subject-centered or existential journey of the traveler, along which various significant key features are marked" (1991: 51–52). Jameson compares the mental images of Lynch's way-finders to those ancient sea charts or *portolans* used for finding harbours, "where coastal features are noted for the use of Mediterranean navigators who rarely venture out into the open sea" (52). Later, with the technological advances of the compass and the sextant, a more complex form of cognitive mapping emerges, as the relationship between the individual and universal or objective conditions—for example, one's position in relation to the stars—would supplement and alter the singular, atomic individual's experiential knowledge. He argues that "[a]t this point, cognitive mapping in the broader sense comes to require the coordination of existential data (the empirical position of the subject) with unlived, abstract conceptions of the geographic totality" (52). Finally, as discussed in Chapter 1, with the advent of the globe in 1490 and the subsequent Mercator projection, "a third dimension of cartography emerges," which according to Jameson occasions a novel crisis of representation, what he calls "the unresolvable (well-nigh Heisenbergian) dilemma of the transfer of curved space to flat charts." The "naïvely" mimetic maps, that is, those in which cartographers have honestly attempted to depict the figured space as "realistically" as possible, are no longer particularly useful, and it rapidly becomes apparent that there can be no "true maps" (52). The Mercator projection, it will be recalled, wilfully distorts the geographical spaces in order to make a more practical map, one that allowed sailors more easily to establish courses using straight lines, even if the sizes of certain places, like Greenland, are grotesquely exaggerated. Jameson asserts that this moment represents a watershed in the history of mapmaking, as the impossibility and undesirability of perfectly mimetic maps opens up the possibility of better and more useful maps, maps which are, it may be added, intentionally figurative or metaphorical.

Jameson's digression on cartography concludes with this consideration of the more practical point: how to "rethink these specialized geographical and cartographic issues in terms of social space," for example, by focusing on "the ways in which we all necessarily *also* cognitively map our individual social relationship to local, national or international class realities" (1991: 52). Indeed, as he later concedes, "'cognitive mapping' was really nothing but a code word for 'class consciousness,'" but of a new kind that could also account for that "new spatiality implicit in the postmodern" (1991: 417–18). However, whether the aim is to represent an unrepresentable international social class or, as Jameson's model makes clear, to situate one's position relative to others in a vast, seemingly unrepresentable social space, a cartographic project is required. Hence Jameson's sense that the Althusserian conception of ideology must also look to the underlying psychoanalytic theory of Jacques Lacan (1901–1981) which had helped to inspire Althusser. Whereas "the Imaginary" and "the Real," as Lacan had called them, are understood and implicit in Althusser's theory of ideology (as imaginary solutions to real contradictions), Jameson notes that Lacan's third element, "the Symbolic," is essential to the project of cognitive mapping. For Lacan, the Imaginary emerges at the "mirror stage," in which the infant is given an illusory coherent image of self. This corresponds in Althusser to the "false consciousness" analysed by Marx in *The German Ideology* (written in 1846), except that in Althusser this process is cognitive; that is, ideology is a way the human subject understands both the world and the self as a coherent entity. The Symbolic order, which for Lacan would be the law of the phallus, is for Althusser entry into the "ideological state apparatuses." For Lacan the Real is unrepresentable but for Althusser it involves the real relations of production. Returning to Jameson, then, the Lacanian or Althusserian order of the Symbolic indicates the intervention of language or the "letter," so this is also the dimension in which literature emerges, and Jameson's concept cognitive mapping can be viewed as a form of literary cartography. Indeed, as Jameson suggests in several places throughout his work, narrative is itself a kind of cognitive mapping, and the crises of representation associated with the modern, and especially postmodern, condition present challenges to the effectiveness and aims of narrative as well as of mapping.

NARRATIVE AND SOCIAL SPACE

Jameson supplements this brief sketch of the history of map-making with an analysis of the different historical productions of space, following Henri Lefebvre, whose theories will be further discussed in Chapter 4. Jameson connects the different organizations of space in history to the various stages of capitalism, as analysed by the economist Ernest Mandel (1923–1995) in his influential book *Late Capitalism* (1975). Jameson moves from a history of the representations of space to the historical production of space, and he focuses on the three stages of capitalist development identified by Mandel: market capitalism, monopoly capitalism or the age of imperialism, and multinational or late capitalism, which Jameson associates with both postmodernism and globalization. He argues that, "The three historical stages of capital have each generated a type of space unique to it, even though these three stages are obviously more profoundly interrelated than are the spaces of other modes of production" (Jameson 1991: 410). Narrative, which is a means of giving expression to experience and of representing reality, responds to, and is affected by, these differing spatial organizations.

As Jameson sees it, the space of market capital is that of the Cartesian grid or the well-ordered city, and it is related to the broader Enlightenment project of secularizing, measuring, and ordering the world. The dominant aesthetic form correlating to this is realism, and the rise of the modern novel is associated with this historical space. Indeed, as with Lukács's discussion of the novel as a form of "transcendental homelessness," Jameson mentions *Don Quixote* in this context. Older forms of meaning and organization evanesce, or rather, are subjugated to the abstractions and disenchantments of geometric space, but this at least makes for a relatively "mappable" social terrain. Realism can enable a sense of place and of spatial relations, even if it must impose the form-giving or sense-making parameters through narrative or aesthetic means.

Later, with the emergence of monopoly capital and imperialism, particularly in the late-nineteenth and early twentieth centuries, a new sort of national space, already becoming international, emerges. As we will argue in the next chapter, the works produced in this period required another level of spatial projection, as the experience of daily life was not really adequate to understand the structures which made possible and conditioned (in the philosophical sense) that experience. As the problem of figuration becomes more urgent, so the techniques associated with modernism (such as stream-of-consciousness, montage, and spatial form) may be viewed as attempts to overcome the representational crisis. As Jameson puts it,

> At this point, the phenomenological experience of the individual subject—traditionally, the supreme raw material of the work of art— becomes limited to a tiny corner of the social world, a fixed-camera view of a certain section of London or the countryside or wherever. But the truth of that experience no longer coincides with the place in which it takes place. The truth of that limited daily experience of London lies, rather, in India or Jamaica or Hong Kong; it is bound up with the whole colonial system of the British Empire that determines the very quality of the individual's subjective life. Yet the structural coordinates are no longer accessible to immediate lived experience and are often not even conceptualizable for most people.
>
> (Jameson 1991: 411)

The paradox, then, is that experience can no longer be both authentic and true, because the material grounds for a person's experience are not apprehensible directly; similarly, the models by which one ascertains the "truth" now elude individual experience. For Jameson, the revolutionary experiments with language and style in modernist texts reflect "an attempt to square this circle and to invent new and elaborate strategies for overcoming this dilemma" (1991: 411).

It is harder to detect the "quantum leap" from this form of nationalist space to the postmodern or global space of late capitalism, but part of the answer lies in the degree to which the national space, that of the "imagined community" as Benedict Anderson so memorably defined a nation (1991), fails to register the utter permeation of capital into formerly undreamed of places. Jameson does not clearly mark the shift, and he suggests that the difference may be one of degree: "If this is so for the age of imperialism, how much more it must hold for our moment" (1991: 412). But with the dismantling of great colonial empires, at least in their most visible forms of direct political control, a sort of withering away of the state has made room for a global or multinational space, thoroughly saturated with capital. Part of this has to do with the "suppression of distance" or "space-time compression," in David Harvey's sense (see 1990: 284–307), that postmodernity and the new technologies of late capitalism have brought with them. The almost instantaneous border crossings and re-crossings, along with the development of seemingly bewildering modes of finance and communication, make for a rather uneasy sense of place in the world.

This postmodern spatial arrangement involves a much greater suppression of distance and saturation of space than earlier historical stages of capital had, but the sense of disorientation and anxiety related to the ever-more-complex spaces and difficulty in mapping them were already apparent at earlier stages. "Cognitive mapping," as Jameson concedes, is really "a more modernist strategy" (1991: 409), and it clearly draws upon elements of Auerbach's sense of figuration, Lukács's totality, and Sartre's existentialism. In his preface to Jameson's *The Geopolitical Aesthetic*, Colin MacCabe has written that the concept of cognitive mapping solved a problem for Jameson's cultural theory: "What Jameson requires is an account of the mechanisms which articulate individual fantasy and social organization" (1992a: xii), and cognitive mapping "is the missing psychology of the political unconscious, the political edge of the historical analysis of postmodernism, and the methodological justification of the Jamesonian undertaking" (1992a: xiv). In defending his own use of cognitive mapping, Jameson has asserted that "the idea has, at least on my view, the advantage of involving the concrete content (imperialism, the world system, subalternity, dependency, and hegemony), while necessarily involving the program of formal analysis of a new kind (since it is centrally defined by the dilemma of representation itself)" (1992a: 188–89). And in the era of globalization, if not also before, many writers and filmmakers "have conceived the vocation of art itself as that of inventing new geotopical cartographies" (Jameson 1992a: 189).

The literary cartographies produced call for methods of reading and interpretation attuned to the spatiality of the narratives. In the next chapter I will discuss several ways in which literary critics have proposed to read such narrative maps and to understand the spaces of literature. As is the case with the figure of Ahab, poring over his charts in his monomaniacal quest for the white whale, often in reading the maps we also find ourselves and our spaces rewritten or remapped.

3

LITERARY GEOGRAPHY

If writers map the real and imagined spaces of their world in various ways through literary means, then it follows that readers are also engaged in this broader mapping project. A map-reader is also a reader of a text, after all, and the reader of a literary map also envisions a space, plots a trajectory, and becomes orientated to and within the world depicted there. What is more, the reader is never simply a passive receptacle for the spatial messages transmitted by the map or text, but actively determines the often shifting and transient meanings to be found in the map. To the writer's literary cartography, we might add the reader's literary geography. The critical reader becomes a kind of geographer who actively interprets the literary map in such a way as to present new, sometimes hitherto unforeseen mappings.

Literary geography also refers to a field of study, and there are a number of scholars actively engaged in it. For example, Barbara Piatti has analysed the geographical spaces of literature in *Die Geographie der Literatur* (2008), and she and her research team are working to produce a literary atlas of Europe, inspired partly by Franco Moretti's call for a literary geography in *Atlas of the European Novel, 1800–1900* (1998), as I discuss later. In my use of the term, however, I mean something a little broader and perhaps more metaphorical. Rather than using actual geographical science or methods such as global-positioning systems to help read the "real-and-imagined" spaces of literature, I am thinking of literary geography as a complement and counterpart to the literary cartographies produced by narratives and other texts. For example, just as literature may be a means of mapping the places represented in a given literary work, the places themselves are deeply imbued with a literary history that has transformed and determined how those places will be "read" or mapped. As the Italian novelist Italo Calvino has observed of Paris,

> a place has to become an inner landscape for the imagination to start to inhabit that place, to turn it into its theatre. Now Paris has already been part of the inner landscape of such a huge part of world literature, of so many books that we have all read, and that have counted in our lives. Before being a city of the real world, Paris for me, as for millions of other people in every country, has been a city that I have imagined through books, a city that you appropriate when you read.
>
> (Calvino 2004: 167)

Paris, not unlike the many books and films set there, is also an imaginary space to be interpreted, a fit subject for literary geography. Literary geography implies a form of reading that focuses attention on space and spatiality in the texts under consideration. But it also means paying attention to the changing spatial or geographical formations that affect literary and cultural productions. This can involve looking at the ways that literature registers the shifting configurations of social space over time, as well as the means by which texts represent or map spaces and places. In a sense, this becomes a matter of shifting from literary history to literary geography, as Moretti has described his own project at times, except that space is also historical, and the history of spatial formations often overlaps with the history of narrative forms. For literary critics and literary historians interested in such overlapping territories, literary geography offers an important means by which to approach the texts. Drawing on the work of selected critics who have actively grappled with questions of spatiality and literature, then, this chapter will examine a spatially oriented reading of literature.

THE SPIRIT OF A PLACE

In *Studies in Classic American Literature* (first published 1923), the British novelist and critic D.H. Lawrence (1885–1930) begins by discussing the "spirit of place," a notion he adapts from the ancient concept of the *genius loci*, a guardian spirit that watches over a particular locale. In Lawrence, the spirit of place combines the quasi-scientific with the quasi-mystical, and he suggests that this "spirit" informs, if not directs and controls, the ideas of the people who live in that place. As he explains,

> Every continent has its own great spirit of place. Every people is polarized in some particular locality, which is home, the homeland. Different places on the face of the earth have different vital effluence, different vibration, different chemical exhalation, different polarity with different stars: call it what you like. But the spirit of place is a great reality.
>
> (Lawrence 1961: 5–6)

Lawrence's use of this concept is intended to explain the character of a people, and in the context of his study, the spirit of place is invoked in order to understand why key nineteenth-century American writers write they way they have. However, it appears that the spirit of place has less to do with how writers map their spaces, that is, with literary cartography, and much more to do with how readers read the works; in other words, the spirit of place is more closely related to literary geography. This is not to say that writers are not also involved in literary geography, only that many readers of literary texts (including, of course, the writers whose work follows from their own readings) engage in a form of map-reading when they approach certain works. The spirit of place is often made visible in the reading of the text.

Lawrence's contemporary, the great English novelist Virginia Woolf (1882–1941) wrote an early review essay on the subject of (and titled) "Literary Geography." In it, Woolf reviews two books, *The Thackeray Country* and *The Dickens Country*, which purport to guide admirers of these famous novelists through those areas of England where the writers had actually been. As Woolf notes, the publisher has included these volumes in its "pilgrimage series," which suggests that the readers will use the texts as guidebooks as they make their own journeys through the physical geography of England in search of the "real" places they already know from the "fictional" depictions of them in the novels of Thackeray or Dickens. Woolf suggests that there are two ways of characterizing the "spirit" in which we are to undertake such a pilgrimage:

> We are either pilgrims from sentiment, who find something stimulating to the imagination in the fact that Thackeray rang this very door bell or that Dickens shaved behind that identical window, or we are scientific in our pilgrimage and visit the country where a great novelist lived in order to see to what extent he was influenced by his surroundings.
>
> (Woolf 1977: 158)

Woolf argues that both motives can be "legitimately satisfied," but that the novelist's depiction of a given locale does not neatly fit with their own biographical connections to the land. To be sure, particularly with writers who are considered "regional" in setting or scope, the reader will more directly associate the author with the people and geography depicted; "Scott's men and women are Scotch; Miss Brontë loves her moors," writes Woolf (1997: 158). But the peregrinations of a young Thackeray and Dickens around England are less valuable to a reader than the adventures of Becky Sharp or David Copperfield.

Woolf concludes that this attempt to draw meaningful connections between the literary cartography of a Dickens or a Thackeray and the physical geography of London is wrongheaded:

> A writer's country is a territory within his own brain; and we run the risk of disillusionment if we try to turn such phantom cities

into tangible brick and mortar. We know our way there without signposts or policemen, and we can greet the passers by without need of introduction. No city indeed is so real as this that we make for ourselves and people to our liking; and to insist that it has any counterpart in the cities of the earth is to rob it of half its charm.

(1977: 161)

For Woolf, then, the reader's desire to visit the real places that appear in the fiction of Thackeray or Dickens results in the diminution of the affective power of the imaginary places established in the writer's, and reader's, own brain.

This is a point made by Umberto Eco in *Six Walks in the Fictional Woods*. As we observed in Chapter 2, Eco admitted to being "one of those who has gone looking for the house in Eccles Street in Dublin where Leopold Bloom [from Joyce's *Ulysses*] is supposed to have lived" (1994: 84). Yet Eco mentions this "episode of literary fanship" only to dismiss its value for criticism or interpretation: "To be a good reader of Joyce, it's not necessary to celebrate Bloomsday on the banks of the Liffey" (84). Eco then provides an instructive and amusing example, using his own 1989 novel *Foucault's Pendulum* to show the absurdity, but also the attractiveness, of confusing the literary space with the geographical sites in which events in a novel take place.

Eco starts by mentioning to what lengths he went in order to ensure the most realistic depiction of the events in his novel. Referring to a scene in which his character Casaubon, at near midnight on June 23–24, 1984, walks the length of the rue Saint-Martin in Paris, Eco explains that, "in order to write this chapter, I walked the same route on several different nights, carrying a tape recorder, taking notes on what I could see and what impressions I had" (1994: 76). Furthermore, Eco made use of a computer program that could "show me what the sky looked like at any time of the year, at whatever latitude and longitude." He even investigated whether the moon was full or not in Paris on this particular evening, and tried to ascertain what position in the sky the moon would have occupied at various times.

In short, Eco admits that he worked very hard to reconstruct the very *real* time and space of the Parisian district he was about to make part of his fictional world.

After *Foucault's Pendulum* was published, Eco received a letter from a reader who wondered why this chapter made no mention of an enormous fire, which occurred nearby that very night in the "real" geospace of Paris and which the Casaubon character could not possibly have missed. The reader, in detecting just how meticulously realistic Eco's narrative purported to be, was perplexed as to why *this* detail, of all the many other details, would have been omitted. "To amuse myself," Eco recounts, "I answered that Casaubon had probably seen the fire but that he hadn't mentioned it for some mysterious reason, unknown to me" (1994: 76–77). Of course, this particular reader may be taking things too far, but Eco uses this anecdote to point out the significant and often complicated relationship between fictional and real spaces. The literary cartography of parts of Paris that Eco had created through language and imagination becomes a text interpreted and analysed by readers who are apt to associate the imaginary places with the ones they might encounter in the city itself.

Eco supplements this example with another: a group of students made a photograph album of all the (real) places that Casaubon visited on his long walk, including "an Oriental bar full of sweating customers, beer kegs, and greasy spits" which these students succeeded in locating and photographing. "It goes without saying that the bar was an invention of mine," Eco notes, "but those two students had undoubtedly discovered the bar described in my book" (1994: 86–87). Eco argues that these students were not wrong in assuming that the novel needed to remain absolutely faithful to the places represented in it, but that they had used fiction to help them get a better sense of the place. As Eco puts it, "they wanted to transform the 'real' Paris into a place in my book, and of all that they could have found in Paris, they chose only those aspects that corresponded to my descriptions" (87). That is, rather than looking at the novel as an imperfect representation of the actual geospace, as perhaps did the reader who was curious about the omitted reference to the fire, these readers used the novel's literary map to revise their own ways of seeing the city itself: "They used the novel to give form to that shapeless and immense universe which the real Paris is" (Eco 1994: 87). Reading, in this sense, is clearly an exercise in literary geography.

With this example we find that the "spirit of place," which was to have influenced or even determined the literature that is produced there, is really more of a power discovered through reading these texts. Obviously, the reading and the writing are complementary, and there is a great deal of overlapping territory in the production and consumption of literature, although literary geography is largely a product of the reader's own engagement with the text, and especially with the narrative maps produced therein. As Eco puts it, "to read fiction means to play a game by which we give sense to the immensity of things that have happened, are happening, or will happen in the actual world" (1994: 87). This is equally true of the spaces as of the events depicted. In reading, the spirit of place emerges from the writer's literary cartography which the reader uses to give imaginative form to the actual world. In so doing, the reader of the narrative maps draws upon frames of reference to help make sense of both the text, the spaces it represents, and the world.

A key frame of reference in modern literary geography is mentioned directly in Woolf's essay, and what seems a parochial distinction at times becomes a device for organizing the spaces of the world-system as a whole. In what could be viewed as a slightly facetious observation about the titles of the books she is reviewing, Woolf writes: "It seems a little incongruous to talk of the Thackeray 'country' or the Dickens 'country' in this way; for the word calls up a vision of woods and fields," whereas in the works of these London-based novelists one could suppose that "the whole world is ... paved with cobble stones" (1977: 158). Here Woolf contrasts the rustic ideals of a country, where the word "country" can denote both a specifically non-urban experience and a kind of national identity, with the cosmopolitan aura of the capital city, whose denizens may not belong to "any recognized type" (159). This distinction between the country and the city goes well beyond simple locations on the map, and comes to determine the ways in which literary geography organizes a reader's sense of the world at large.

THE COUNTRY AND THE CITY

Raymond Williams (1921–1988), the influential British literary critic and cultural historian, is generally thought to be among the founders of cultural studies, and his multifaceted investigations of literature helped to change the way that literary studies were imagined. In one of his most famous works, *The Country and the City* (1973), Williams explores the conceptual dichotomy as it appears across some 350 years of British literature, from the pastoral idylls of seventeenth-century poetry to the modernist writings of the twentieth century, with theoretical excurses into Marxist criticism and cultural materialism. In his thorough and nuanced study, Williams establishes the changing valences of these terms and the ideas they represent, and he demonstrates how literature embodies what he calls "**structures of feeling**" associated with places and spaces.

Williams begins his study by noting how forceful, yet complicated, these terms are.

> "Country" and "city" are very powerful words, and this is not surprising when we remember how much they seem to stand for in the experience of human communities. In English, "country" is both a nation and a part of the "land"; "the country" can be the whole society or its rural area. In the long history of human settlements, this connection between the land from which directly or indirectly we all get our living and the achievements of human society has been deeply known. And one of these achievements has been the city: the capital, the large town, a distinctive form of civilisation.
>
> (1973: 1)

In some ways, one could argue that Williams's lengthy study of "the country" and "the city" is a more elaborate version of the "keywords" he would assemble a few years later, designed to help students and critics make sense of the shifting terminology necessary to study culture and society. In *Keywords* (1976),

Williams would define terms in an effort to show how meanings had changed over time and how supplementary significance became attached to such terms. In *The Country and the City*, one can see a fullest exposition of the process, albeit limited for the most part in the earlier book to British literary and cultural history.

Williams notes with some amusement that the nostalgia for a simpler past, one typified by a rustic "organic community," always seemed to locate that past "just back, we can see, over the last hill" (1973: 9). That is, writers complaining of the loss of this "organic community" felt always that the breakdown of such community was a recent occurrence, but Williams shows that while contemporary criticism felt that this change had occurred since the First World War, it was really echoing the thoughts of earlier writers, who located the moment of transformation in the 1890s, the 1830s, or the 1770s. Indeed, Williams notes complaints over the loss of "Old England" and "its timeless agri-cultural rhythms" extending back to Thomas More's *Utopia* (1516) or even to William Langland's *Piers Plowman* in the 1370s (10–11). Seemingly, this pastoral ideal extends all the way back to Eden, where each occasion for nostalgic longing is but another way to bemoan the present status quo. But, as he then makes clear, "Old England, settlement, rural virtues—all these, in fact, mean different things at different times" (12), and the analysis of the country versus the city will require a nuanced reading.

To engage in this reading, Williams invokes what he calls "structures of feeling." In *Marxism and Literature* (1977), he characterizes this term by distinguishing the somewhat woolly sounding "feeling" from concepts like "world-view" or "ideology": "we are concerned with meanings and values as they are actively lived and felt, and the relations between these and formal or systematic beliefs are in practice variable (including historically variable)." Such elements of feeling constitute a "structure," that is, "a set, with specific internal relations, at once interlocking and in tension" (1977: 132). For Williams, then, the shifting structures of feeling of a given group at a particular time and in a particular place can enable readers to understand the emergence of new modes of experience.

In *The Country and the City*, we can see that the changing views of the pastoral or rustic "Old England" and the new cultural apprehension of emerging towns, cities, and the metropolis involve complex and nuanced shifts in the structure of feeling within a population at a particular moment. However, as Williams warns, a structure of feeling involves "social experience still *in process*, often indeed not yet recognized as social, but taken to be private, idiosyncratic, even isolating, but which in analysis (and rarely otherwise) has its emergent, connecting, and dominant characteristics" (1977: 132). Indeed, one could say that a given structure of feeling is only truly recognizable as such by a reader after a new structure of feeling has emerged. Although the term may seem both too vague and too broad for concrete, Marxian analysis, and Williams himself later regretted its unintended comprehensiveness, a "structure of feeling" does allow one to examine the complex inter-relations of literary forms and social experience (see Williams 1981: 164).

The shifting sense of the urban experience, particularly with respect to the metropolis of London, offers a good example. Unlike the new industrial towns of the eighteenth and nineteenth centuries, which tended to be organized around a single industry or type of workplace, London's vast "miscellaneity and randomness in the end embodied a system" (1973: 154). In his consideration of Charles Dickens as an exemplar of the new urban writer, Williams shows how "Dickens's creation of a new kind of novel [...] can be directly related to what we must see as this double condition: the random and the systematic, the visible and the obscured, which is the true significance of the city, and especially at this period of the capital city, as a dominant social form" (154). With Dickens, the novel itself becomes a kind of narrative map of the city of London, where the heterogeneity and multitude of persons and of places are somehow interconnected and made sensible through the novel. As Williams puts it, "the experience of the city is the fictional method; or the fictional method is the experience of the city" (154). In Dickens, the very form of the urban novel, rather than the topography or setting or other empirical data, makes possible the literary cartography of London.

Williams then discusses what he calls "knowable communities," and he suggests that a kind of "fiction of the city" would differ from the "fiction of the country," insofar as the novelistic depiction of "experience and community would be essentially opaque" in the city kind, but "essentially transparent" in the country type (165). As Williams puts it,

> the transition from country to city—from a predominantly rural to a predominantly urban society—is transforming and significant. The growth of towns and especially of cities and a metropolis; the increasing division and complexity of labour; the altered and critical relations between and within social classes: in changes like these any assumption of a knowable community—a whole community, wholly knowable—became harder and harder to sustain.
>
> (1973: 165)

Williams's analysis here already points to the conditions under which the need for a Kevin Lynch-styled "imageable" city comes into being, and the perpetual nostalgia for a simpler time, just over the horizon behind us, has much to do with the perception of lost "knowability."

But it is also true that in the nineteenth century there comes into being what the sociologist Lyn H. Lofland has called "the world of strangers," in which "the people to be found within its boundaries at a given moment know nothing personally about the vast *majority* of others with whom they share this space" (1973: 3). Yet this unknowably urban space also makes possible opportunities and mobility that was previously undreamed of. The experience of the individual in the large city forms a key point of reference for modern literature, and the "man of the crowd," as Edgar Allan Poe labelled one mysterious character, is explored by a number of different writers interested in exploring this social dynamic. As Williams notes, "this experience, clearly, could go either way: into an affirmation of common humanity, past the barriers of crowded strangeness; or into an emphasis of isolation, of mystery—an ordinary feeling that can become a terror" (234). The novels of Dickens, for instance, might tend towards the former, whereas a writer like Fyodor Dostoevsky, in such works as *Notes from the Underground* or *Crime and Punishment*, could emphasize the strangeness and disconnectedness of individuals in the city. In the work of the French poet and critic Charles Baudelaire, the two tendencies are intertwined, as the "isolation and loss of connection were the conditions of a new and lively perception" (Williams 1973: 234).

As Williams's study demonstrates, the dichotomy of country and city emerged as a model for imagining the British nation-state, among others, and it eventually becomes a model for imagining the entire world-system. As Williams says, once the term *metropolitan* can be used to describe whole societies and *underdeveloped* can stand for largely agricultural or non-industrialized societies, "a model of city and country, in economic and political relationships, has gone beyond the boundaries of the nation-state, and is seen but also challenged as a model for the world" (279). Thus, "one of the last models of 'city and country' is the system we now know as imperialism" (279).

THE CENTRALITY OF THE PERIPHERY

As Williams's concluding remarks to *The Country and the City* suggest, the structures of feeling in an age of globalization must in some ways account for the multinational world system, which is also to say, such structures must address the fact and legacies of a vast colonial network and its effects. In this section, I want to examine the implication of this by looking at cultural interrelations between the **core** and the **periphery**, to use the terms of the American sociologist Immanuel Wallerstein (1930–). In particular, I will look at the work of Palestinian-born American literary critic Edward Said (1935–2003), who demonstrates the "overlapping territories" of literature and empire in such writings as *Orientalism* (1978) and *Culture and Imperialism* (1993). Said shows how what had seemed literally and figuratively peripheral, such as the goings-on in distant lands far from the metropolitan centres of London or Paris, are actually central to the formation of literature and culture in Great Britain, France, and the United States.

As Williams points out, the rapid developments of the capitalist political economy in the nineteenth century required continuous expansion of markets well beyond the domestic space of the nation-state. "The traditional relationship between city and country was then thoroughly rebuilt on an international scale" (1973: 280). In some respects, the basic city-versus-country dichotomy, perhaps with the addition of a "suburban" inter-mediary space, parallels the tripartite division among periphery, core, and **semiperiphery** made famous by Wallerstein. In *The Modern World System*, Volume I, Wallerstein writes:

> World-economies are divided into core-states and peripheral areas. I do not say peripheral *states* because one characteristic of a peripheral area is that the indigenous state is weak, ranging from its nonexistence (that is, a colonial situation) to one with a low degree of autonomy (that is, a neo-colonial situation).
>
> There are also semiperipheral areas which are in between the core and the periphery on a series of dimensions, such as the complexity of economic activities, strength of the state machinery, cultural integrity, etc. Some of these areas had been core-areas of earlier versions of a given world-economy. Some had been peripheral areas that were later promoted, so to speak, as a result of the changing geopolitics of an expanding world-economy.
>
> (1974: 349)

Wallerstein's distinction does not separate these spatio-political zones, however, as he notes the ways in which all three interact. As Said and other commentators will make clear, the political and economic interrelations are supplemented by literary and cultural ones.

In *Orientalism*, Said shows how the "imaginative geography" represents different spaces and types of space according to the rather arbitrary distinctions made by individuals or groups. As he puts it, the "practice of designating in one's mind a familiar space which is 'ours' and an unfamiliar space which is 'theirs' is a way of making geographical distinctions that can be quite arbitrary. [...] It is enough for 'us' to set up these boundaries in our own minds; 'they' become 'they' accordingly, and both their territory and their mentality are designated as different from 'ours'" (1978: 54). Drawing upon Gaston Bachelard's arguments in *The Poetics of Space* (which I will discuss in the next chapter), Said then notes that "space acquires emotional and even rational sense by a kind of poetic process, whereby the vacant and anonymous reaches of distance are converted into meaning for us here" (55). Just as the "country" and the "city" emerged, in different ways, as models for organizing the domestic spaces of Great Britain (and, eventually, the world), the ancient dichotomy of "our land–barbarian land" translates into a basic structure with which to organize the spaces of one's imaginative geography. For Said, this lies at the heart of the orientalism (and, more broadly, a certain attitude towards all peripheral zones) that develops in European culture. A good literary example of the interplay can be found in J.M. Coetzee's novel *Waiting for the Barbarians*, which deals in detail with questions of distance and proximity, and where the perspective changes as the distance varies.

In *Culture and Imperialism*, Said engages in what he calls "a kind of geographical inquiry into historical experience," and he takes as a starting point that "none of us is completely free from the struggle over geography," a struggle that is not only about imperial armies and direct conquest, but also "about ideas, about forms, about images and imaginings" (1993: 7). Indeed, narrative is as much the contested "territory" that Said wishes to explore as the physical spaces of the earth. As he observes,

> The main battle in imperialism is over land, of course; but when it came to who owned the land, who had the right to settle and work on it, who kept it going, who won it back, and who now plans its future—these issues were reflected, contested, and even for a time decided in narrative.
>
> (xiii)

Drawing upon these surmises and discoveries, Said boldly proclaims that imperialism is the "determining, political horizon of modern Western culture" (1993: 60).

Said attempts to update Williams's notion of structures of feeling with the less elegant but perhaps more accurate phrase, "**structures of attitude and reference**" (1993: 52). Said finds that nineteenth- and early twentieth-century novels exhibit this structure of attitude and reference with respect to territorial empire, and that this sometimes leads to surprising interpretative findings. For example, Said discovers that the more overt novelistic references to empire, in the works of Conrad or Kipling, are really of a piece with earlier, but not as explicit, narratives of Austen, Thackeray, or Dickens, where British imperialism is not the subject but part of the ideological sub-structure of the novels. As Said observes, "both the formal characteristics and the contents of all these novelists' works belong to the same cultural formation" (75).

Said goes further than merely suggesting the interrelations of empire and cultural texts: He insists that "[w]ithout empire, I would go so far as saying, there is no European novel as we know it" (69). Clearly, the profit motive inspired the expansion of colonial empires, but Said emphasizes the cultural aspects of imperialism (which is distinct from, though obviously related to colonialism), that "allowed decent men and women to accept the notion that distant territories and their native peoples *should* be subjugated" and "these decent people could think of the *imperium* as a protracted, almost metaphysical obligation to rule subordinate, inferior, or less advanced peoples" (7). In his examination of the topic in *Geographical Imaginations*, Derek Gregory alludes to this as "dispossession by othering" (1994: 179), whereby a "they" can be deemed unfit to govern themselves, which allows the colonizers to adopt the humanitarian stance of the "civilizing mission," where it becomes the duty of those in the metropolitan centre to "look out for" their colonized populations in the periphery.

Said points out that the so-called "age of empire" coincides neatly with "the period in which the novel form and the new historical narrative become preeminent," but he insists that "most cultural historians, and certainly all literary scholars, have failed to remark the *geographical* notation, the theoretical mapping and charting of territories that underlies Western fiction, historical writing, and philosophical discourse of the time" (58). A proper analysis would require greater attention to the spatiality of empire, to the geographical and cartographical aspects of the imperial mission and its multifarious effects. An example of the type of work Said has in mind can be found in Paul Carter's magnificent book, *The Road to Botany Bay: An Essay in Spatial History* (1987), in which he explores the polyvalent uses of myth, history, geography, and mapping in the colonization of Australia.

In a note on modernism, Said suggests that the new aesthetic forms reflect a growing apprehension of the irony of imperialism, of the overlapping territories of the "other" in the metropolitan centres, or of what Marlowe in Joseph Conrad's *Heart of Darkness* (originally published in 1899) enunciated when noting that "this also has been one of the dark places on the earth," thus showing how Europe's supposed superiority is itself contingent and ephemeral. "To deal with this," writes Said, "a new encyclopedic form became necessary," and the features of the modernist novel would include "a circularity of structure, inclusive and open at the same time," (as, for example, in the stream-of-consciousness of Joyce's *Ulysses*), and whose "novelty [is] based on a reformulation of old, even outdated fragments drawn self-consciously from disparative locations, sources, and cultures." Such techniques would also include epic and mythic elements, not to mention generic and pop-cultural elements, and an "irony of a form that draws attention to itself as substituting art and its creations for the once-possible synthesis of the world empires" (1994: 189). Indeed, what Joseph Frank identified as the "spatial form" in modern literature (1991) coincides nicely with Said's argument here, as literary artists endeavoured to "say everything at once," perhaps, by freezing time in the moment of simultaneity. In this discussion, Said's position is similar to Jameson's sense that the age of imperialism or of monopoly capitalism brought about a schism between "truth" and "experience," where the truth of one's London-based experience lay in Jamaica or India or elsewhere (as we saw in Chapter 2). However, for Said, this aesthetic of modernism was a reaction to the impending breakdown of the imperial system, as the artist attempted to hold an imaginary reality together which was no longer feasible in the "real world." As Said concludes, "Spatiality becomes, ironically,

the characteristic of an aesthetic rather than of political domination, as more and more regions—from India to Africa to the
Caribbean—challenge the classical empires and their cultures"
(190).

The centrifugal forces of cultural power that make possible the
imperial system Said analyses are in some respects matched by
the centripetal forces than draw everything back to a centralized
hub. As in both Williams's and Said's studies, the metropolis or
large, often capital, city emerges as its own kind of spatial and
cultural entity, different from the typical town or city by virtue of
its centrality in a world system. By the late twentieth century,
for instance, the Dutch sociologist Saskia Sassen (1949–) could
identify London, New York, and Tokyo, among a few others, as
"global cities" (1991), which are undoubtedly still crucial to their
national economies but which have exceeding the political
and economic boundaries of the nation-states in which they are
situated. The experience within the city becomes a key element
for the literary geography of modern and postmodern cultural
spaces.

THE PERAMBULATIONS OF THE *FLÂNEUR*

In his combined studies and experiences of Paris which appear in
his immense, incomplete, and posthumously published *Arcades
Project* (1999), the German cultural critic Walter Benjamin
(1892–1940) established the *flâneur* as the archetypically modern
figure. The *flâneur* is the idle, urban stroller, one who tarries
almost as much as he moves, the window-shopper or voyeur, the
man of the crowd who refuses to be part of the crowd. Benjamin's
reflections on the figure of the *flâneur* arise from his consideration
of the urban poetry of Charles Baudelaire (1821–1867), who
describes the figure in his essay "The Painter of Modern Life." For
Benjamin to discover the emblematic representative of modernity
in this idle stroller, then, is an odd choice, but it points to the
significance of urban space and movement in this view of
the modern world.

The *flâneur*'s distinctiveness from the mere rambler or stroller
lies in his urbanity, but the knowledge of the city inheres not

only in a critical awareness of its differences from non-urban spaces. It also embodies a clear sense of the different forces and effects of a city, and these are often rendered most evident through observing urban populations. Demographic knowledge is nearly as crucial as geographic knowledge, and the mobile psychology of metropolitan populations is a key aspect of both Baudelaire's and Benjamin's social and literary criticism. For Baudelaire, the most important thinker of this condition is actually a poet, Edgar Allan Poe. In his own life and works, Poe takes to the streets, scouting out the "urban island, a sea within the middle of the sea," to use a phrase that the French philosopher and historian Michel de Certeau (1925–1986) used to describe Manhattan in *The Practice of Everyday Life* (1984: 91). Poe, along with certain of his characters and like Baudelaire's *flâneur*, eschews the more comprehensive vision afforded by the narrative overview.

In his speculative analysis of "walking in the city" (which I examine further in the next chapter), de Certeau distinguishes between the street-level view of the pedestrian or window-shopper and the panoptic overview afforded by looking down upon the city from a great height, his example of which is the observation deck of the then newly constructed World Trade Center in New York City. The latter vantage creates a god's-eye view that presumes to *know* the city, whereas the pedestrian actually *writes* the city in "a long poem of walking" (1984: 101). The influential German sociologist Georg Simmel (1858–1918), in his essay entitled "The Metropolis and Mental Life," points out that "the psychological basis of the metropolitan type of individuality consists in the *intensification of nervous stimulation* which results from the swift and uninterrupted change of outer and inner stimuli" (1950: 409–10) That is, the perceptual bombardment of mobile and protean phenomena that characterizes daily life in the big city alters a given individual's fundamental physiological and cognitive processes. In Poe's short story "The Man of the Crowd," the title character, as well as the narrator who unsuccessfully attempts to understand him, become representative figures of this intensification, and in constantly walking in the city, they are fundamentally *displaced* at all times.

Yet, in Baudelaire's figure of the *flâneur* and in Benjamin's reading of it, this intensification and displacement are also elements of the pleasant "electricity," where the man of the crowd is "a reservoir of electric energy" (Benjamin 1969: 175).

In "The Painter of Modern Life," Baudelaire characterizes the *flâneur* as a man of the crowd; however, although Baudelaire's model may derive from Poe's tale, it is not the title character, but the narrator who observes, describes, and investigates the inscrutable psychology of the man of the crowd, who is really more like a *flâneur*, a point made by Benjamin in his rereading. Benjamin says, "The man of the crowd is no *flâneur*. In him, composure has given way to manic behavior. Hence, he exemplifies, rather, what had to become of the *flâneur* once he was deprived of the milieu to which he belonged" (1969: 172). Benjamin distinguishes between "the pedestrian who would let himself be jostled by the crowd" and "the *flâneur* who demanded elbow room"; the latter "can indulge in the perambulations of the *flâneur* only if as such he is already out of place" (172).

In addition to Poe, Baudelaire's inspiration for his idea of the *flâneur* comes from the French artist, Constantin Guys; in considering Guys's painting, Baudelaire presents a broader explanation of the *flâneur*'s definitive characteristics:

> The crowd is his element, as the air is that of birds and water of fishes. His passion and his profession are to become one flesh with the crowd. For the perfect *flâneur*, for the passionate spectator, it is an immense joy to set up house in the heart of the multitude, amid the ebb and flow of movement, in the midst of the fugitive and infinite. To be away from home and yet to feel oneself everywhere at home; to see the world, to be at the centre of the world, and yet to remain hidden from the world—such are a few of the slightest pleasures of those independent, passionate, impartial natures which the tongue can but clumsily define. The spectator is a *prince* who everywhere rejoices in his incognito. The lover of life makes the whole world his family, just like the lover of the fair sex who builds up his family from all the beautiful women that he has ever found, or that are—or are not—to be found; or the lover of pictures who lives in a magical society of dreams painted on canvas. Thus the lover of

universal life enters into the crowd as though it were an immense reservoir of electrical energy. Or we might liken him to a mirror as vast as the crowd itself; or to a kaleidoscope gifted with consciousness, responding to each one of its movements and reproducing the multiplicity of life and the flickering grace of all the elements of life. He is an "I" with an insatiable appetite for the "non-I," at every instant rendering and explaining it in pictures more living than life itself, which is always unstable and fugitive.

(Baudelaire 1964: 9–10)

As the phrase "kaleidoscope gifted with consciousness" suggests, the images produced are likely to be both strange and beautiful, but perhaps they do not offer a clear basis for knowledge of the city. The "world" thus represented is not really a world to be known, but a plenum to be experienced in various, often unsettling ways.

Baudelaire understood immediately that the key aspect of Poe's or of Guys's genius lay not in discovering a hitherto unknown entity, but in approaching reality from a particular point of view and thereby seeing things very differently. For Baudelaire, the novel way of seeing was obviously artistic, but it was also far more than that. It requires what Baudelaire calls "a *man of the world* [...] a man who understands the world and the mysterious and lawful reasons for all of its uses," and Baudelaire cites Poe's "Man of the Crowd" to make his point. Notably, he focuses on the narrator of that story, rather than the "man of the crowd" himself, to define the type of artist that can really be the man of the world. As Baudelaire summarizes,

In the window of a coffee-house there sits a convalescent, pleasurably absorbed in gazing at the crowd, and mingling, through the medium of thought, in the turmoil of thought that surrounds him. But lately returned from the valley of the shadow of death, he is rapturously breathing in all the odours and essences of life; as he has been on the brink of total oblivion, he remembers, and fervently desires to remember, everything. Finally he hurls himself headlong into the midst of the throng, in pursuit of the unknown, half-glimpsed

countenance that has, on an instant, bewitched him. Curiosity has a
become fatal, irresistible passion.

(1964: 7)

The man of the world is not, therefore, the man of the
crowd. The man of the world, here represented by Poe's
convalescent and extremely curious narrator, is a "passionate
spectator." However, this kaleidoscope equipped with consciousness is not the social scientist that the narrator had imagined
himself to be at the beginning of the tale, but an uncertain,
mobile registrar of the unknowable.

With Benjamin's rereading of Baudelaire's reading of Poe,
there emerge a new aesthetic sensibility with respect to urban
space, and social space more generally. For these writers, "knowing" gives way to different types of experience, such that the
perambulating *flâneur* is less a wayfinding cartographer, like
Kevin Lynch's urban inhabitants, and more of an artist or poet
of the streets, someone who "paints" modern life in its abstract
and shifting imagery. Such an approach to the interrelations of
literary art and social space presents the opportunity for new
and different readings, as for example in Kirsten Ross's study *The
Emergence of Social Space: Rimbaud and the Paris Commune* (1988).
Taken together these ideas prompt a reconsideration of literary
history in terms of the spaces of literature.

NOVEL SPACES FOR LITERARY HISTORY

The analysis of spatial practices and historical spaces allows us to
recognize the degree to which literary texts both operate within
and help to shape the geography of their worlds, and through
them, of ours. In their literary cartography, texts give form to a
world that makes it real, while also making sense of that world
in an allegorical structure of meaning that enables the reader to
generate alternative meanings. The interplay of these various
meanings establishes a constellation in which the various data of
lived experience are mapped onto a greater plane of significance,
such that the lived and the unlived become visible in a useful,
albeit provisional, form. As Frank Kermode notes, the task of the

critic is a lesser, but still important one: "making sense of the ways we try to make sense of our lives" (1967: 3). This is, in part, the task of a literary geography. In this section, I want to focus on one scholar's bold attempt to re-imagine the literary history of the novel in terms of spatiality or of literary geography.

In recent decades, the Italian literary critic Franco Moretti has sought to redefine literary history and the historiographic practices employed by it. Recently, he has given new emphasis to the concept of "world literature" and he has attempted to develop tools for approaching this vast subject. At stake in his re-evaluation is a new way of reading. Moretti's approach is not ahistorical; his readings are still grounded in a historical and historicist practice that examines individual texts and the forms that they represent in the time of their emergence and proliferation. However, Moretti endeavours to alter the historicist practices to encompass a new way of looking at literature: specifically, he is interested in the spaces of literature in the world. As he intimated in *Modern Epic*, this would require a "literary geography" (1996: 76).

Geography in Moretti's work is both literal and metaphorical. In its literal meaning, especially as elaborated in *The Atlas of the European Novel, 1800–1900* (1998) and *Graphs, Maps, Trees: Abstract Models for a Literary History* (2005), Moretti's literary geography involves three distinct literary critical activities: first, he examines the interplay of narrative and "real" spaces, like Dickens's London or Balzac's Paris, focusing on how novelists represent the space of the city, region, nation, and world; second, in addition to discussing how novels or other literary forms represent space, Moretti also looks at how these forms themselves circulate in space, through a literary marketplace and the various geographical domains (e.g. local, regional, national) in which reading and writing occur; and finally, he adapts to this geographical project a new way of reading individual texts, by plotting in the form of a diagram, or on an actual map, discrete elements of a text that will provide the foundation for a reading. Hence, mapping becomes a literary critical practice in itself, while also producing tools for further analysis.

As a metaphor, Moretti's literary geography stands as a figure for a new science of literary history, where the "mapping project" connotes an epistemological program, as, for example, when one *surveys* a field of knowledge. Moretti's new science, which often announces itself in relation to already constituted social or natural scientific fields, such as sociology, quantitative history, biology, and geography itself, promotes a model of literary history that can be grasped according to discernible laws or at least recognizable trends. Literary geography is not really the name for this new science, but geographical language provides a certain vocabulary for understanding the phenomena Moretti is describing. The deployment of this geographical model has far-reaching effects. As Michel Foucault has observed, "Once knowledge can be analysed in terms of region, domain, implantation, displacement, transposition, one is able to capture the process by which knowledge functions as a form of power and disseminates the effects of power" (1980b: 69). Following from this, one can reasonably claim that the new literary history or literary geography established by Moretti opens up a new space for examining the power of literature as an institution.

There are at least three levels at which Moretti's literary-historical mapping project operates. First, he envisions a kind of mapping of individual literary texts, schematizing them or plotting their courses on actual maps as a way of reading them. Such a way of reading yields new information about the text, and so becomes a supplemental interpretative method in addition to the process of interpreting the words on the page. Second, Moretti is interested in redefining the theory and practice of literary history, moving beyond the chronicle of individual texts, styles, or movements, and projecting a new science of literature that itself is, at least in part, geographical as much as it is historical. And third, Moretti wants his mapping project to actively constitute the field rather than merely to study it. That is, Moretti's project aims at constructing a field of discourse, with multiple authors and texts, that will present a new image of the world of literature. His grand project on *The Novel* (2006), whose two large volumes in English are reduced from five volumes in the Italian original, is the provisional result of this latter aim.

Before examining Moretti's specific revisionary strategy, it is useful to look at the perceived problem that he has with existing practices of literary criticism and history. Moretti believes that literary history has largely failed to do its job of surveying the field, primarily because traditional literary history has not attempted to examine the vast array of literature. He finds the practice of literary history, and literary studies more generally, to lack the scientific rigour necessary to fully understand its object of study. For example, by focusing only on a canon of particularly valued texts, Moretti complains, scholars have ignored the many hundreds of thousands of other texts in existence. His criticisms, revised and updated throughout his career, have also been remarkably consistent, in evidence as early as *Signs Taken for Wonders* (1983), when he condemned the "historiographical status of literary criticism."

> Tottering and obsolete in this respect, literary history has never ceased to be *histoire évenementialle*, where the "events" are great works or great individuals. Even the great historical controversies, when all is said, turn almost exclusively on the reinterpretation of an extremely small number of works and authors. This procedure condemns the concept of genre to a subaltern, marginal function, as is indicated most starkly in the formalist couple convention-defamiliarization, where genre appears as mere *background*, an opaque plane whose only use is to make the *difference* of the master-piece more prominent. Just as the "event" breaks and ridicules the laws of continuity, so the masterpiece is there to demonstrate the "triumph" over the norm, the irreducibility of what is really great.
>
> (1983: 13)

Here Moretti identifies the unscientific character of literary criticism and history. Rather than describing literature in general, the emergence of literary forms, the characteristics that allow them to cohere, the way they circulate, and the forces that allow them to persist or that drive them into oblivion, literary history returns to the anomalous, the singular, or the exception to whatever rule might be presupposed if not established. For Moretti, such a science cannot be true; a literary history that looks less at norms and more at anomalies cannot give an accurate picture of what literature really is, how it operates, or what effects it has. By focusing on the exceptional, the remarkable, the fascinating, and the odd, literary history has forgotten the normal, ordinary, everyday literature that comprises the vast majority of texts. The landscape painted by traditional literary history, as Moretti sees it, is filled with dizzying peaks and valleys. In its stead, Moretti calls for a "flatter, more boring literature" (1998: 150).

There are a number of immediate consequences that follow from this observation for the study of literature. Without directly speaking to particular debates in relation to any literary canon, Moretti expands considerably the number of texts considered worthy of study. However, to call this an expansion of the canon is not really to do Moretti justice. He is not simply interested in expanding the canon to make it more representative or to chip away at the existing hierarchy of literary works. Moretti may very well want to see a more representative selection of literary works and authors, but his goal is not primarily reform of the existing canon. Rather, he is interested in establishing a clearer field of vision, which will necessarily be broader in scope. This will clearly mean more books, but also different types of books. For example, in *Signs Taken for Wonders*, Moretti wants to show that the study of "mass" or "low" literature, particularly in putatively subliterary genres like detective fiction or horror, can alter the way we look at "great" literature, and will allow literary historians "to reconstruct the literary system of the past with great theoretical precision and historical fidelity" (1983: 16).

Of course, Moretti is less interested in expanding the canon than he is in eliminating the idea of a canon at all, at least for the purposes of his new form of literary history. For him, "the aim is not so much to change the canon—the discovery of precursors to the canon or alternatives to it, to be restored to a prominent position—as change in how we look at *all* of literary history, canonical and noncanonical, together" (2000b: 207–8). Moretti also notes here that he does not "really believe that professors can change the canon" and that, even if they could do so by adding hundreds of new texts, well over 99 per cent of literature would still remain among the "great unread." Hence, the "canon" is not a particularly useful category for looking at the overall field of literary history, although it is obviously useful in establishing what to read when resources are limited. "In households with only one book," Moretti notes, "we find religion; in libraries with only one bookcase, the canon" (1998: 150). The existence of a canon is itself a sign of the growth and diffusion of literature in the real world.

Aside from enlarging the library, Moretti's literary geography attempts to understand the sheer size of the literary marketplace itself. As Moretti has noted in his defence of the practice of "distant reading" (about which I will have more to say later), even the most wide-ranging, broad-minded reader cannot possibly read all of the books that have been produced. Indeed, even limiting oneself to a distinct period of a single national literature, it would be difficult to read everything. As he explains in *Graphs, Maps, Trees*, "a canon of two hundred novels, for instance, sounds very large for nineteenth-century Britain (and *is* much larger than the current one), but it is still less than one per cent of the novels actually published; twenty thousand, thirty, more, no one really knows" (2005: 4). As he moves further down the road towards establishing his new form of literary history, Moretti will, it would appear, necessarily move away from reading the individual texts.

Another consequence of Moretti's turn away from traditional literary history's monumental historiography, to use Nietzsche's phrase, is the emphasis that he places on genre. In order to identify the norm, he must embrace the typical; thus Moretti focuses attention less on individual literary works than on *types* of literary works. He has always been interested in genre, since this concept combines the synchronic and diachronic aspects of literary history. That is, genres develop, evolve, proliferate, and eventually wither away in the course of history, but a genre is also a synchronic element of that history, an integrated form that more or less holds its shape throughout its history. The idea of genre is more than just a tool among others that can be used for Moretti's new literary history. It is the essential form for such history. The "flatter, more boring literature" he wants to embrace is made possible by use of the concept of genre in producing the literary history:

> A history of literature built round this concept will be both "slower" and more "discontinuous" than the one we are familiar with. Slower, because the idea of literary *genre* itself requires emphasis on what a set of works have in *common*. It presupposes that literary production takes place in obedience to a prevailing system of laws and that the task of criticism is precisely to show the extent of their coercive, regulating power.
>
> (1983: 12)

The discontinuity of such history comes, it is claimed, from the defining characteristics of the genres examined. That is, rather than using broad categories based on styles (e.g. romanticism, naturalism, modernism), the lifetimes of individual authors, extra-literary historical events, or the totalizing notion of *Zeitgeist*, Moretti suggests that the internal structures of genres will allow for "more rigid" historical markers. Using the sort of scientific discourse that typifies his mapping project as a whole, Moretti proclaims that the "history of literature must aim to represent its own object as a kind of magnetic field whose overall equilibrium or disequilibrium is only the resultant of the individual forces acting within it" (1983: 16).

A flatter, more boring literature, then, will identify a much larger field of study while focusing on typical or generic literary productions. Although a capable, indeed elegant reader of diverse texts, Moretti has recently established that the type of literary history he is proposing cannot really be accomplished through careful readings. His more recent call for a "distant reading" (2000a), a method he deems most appropriate for attending to the problem of world literature, actually fits in well with the project announced in 1983 in *Signs Taken for Wonders*. The line of argument that almost unwaveringly maintains itself in Moretti's work is that literary history fails to do its job when it fails to grasp fully its entire field of study. With *Graphs, Maps, Trees*, Moretti proceeds to lay out the theoretical argument, to describe the methods, and to supply the tools (or abstract models) for his mapping project.

In "The Slaughterhouse of Literature" (2000b), Moretti had identified a key problem for a literary history that prevents it from truly representing its own object: there is just too much of it. One simply cannot *know* twenty thousand texts. "A larger literary history requires other skills: sampling; statistics; work with series, titles, concordances, incipits" (2000b: 208–9). He also indicates that such skills will require collaboration, a salutary move away from the cleric-like isolated close reader bent over the sacred text, and towards a collective project of knowledge production not unlike cartography, in fact. Indeed, venturing far from the safe shores of the liberal humanities, this will require exploration of the uncharted seas of quantitative analysis, since "quantitative work is truly *cooperative*: not only in the pragmatic sense that it takes forever to gather the data, but because such data are ideally independent from any individual researcher, and can thus be shared by others, and combined in more than one way" (2005: 5). The gathering, organizing, and analysing of data will be essential for the sort of literary history Moretti aims to produce.

Moretti's idea for a distant reading of literature is laid out in his "Conjectures on World Literature" (2000a). In order to grasp the field, "literary history will quickly become very different from what it is now: it will become 'second hand': a patchwork of other people's research, *without a single direct textual reading*" (2000a: 57). Rather than reading individual texts, the distant reader will examine other units, "much smaller or much larger than the text: devices, themes, tropes—or genres and systems" (2000a: 57). Distant reading, therefore, is not a supplementary approach to close reading, but a new kind of literary history entirely. In order to achieve this, the old tools of criticism are no longer of much use. This is also a spatialization of the field of literary history, such that it can be surveyed more broadly and effectively, at least from Moretti's point of view.

The experiment would appear to involve ways of perceiving literature without actually reading the texts. In *Graphs, Maps, Trees*, Moretti provides the "abstract models" for such an approach. Using quantitative research from various sources, graphs can be made that will offer a distant reader a bird's-eye view of the rise and fall of various genres; by plotting elements of a text on a diagram, maps provide a new look at the way literary spaces are represented and experienced; and, by graphically showing the dead ends and the continuing lines of literary conventions, trees provide a model for the "evolution" of literary forms. Each model allows the distant reader to examine different facets of the literary field, and each involves a form of explanation that minimizes the process of interpretation. As Moretti points out, the models "share a clear preference for explanation over interpretation; or perhaps, better, for the explanation of general structures over the interpretation of individual texts" (2005: 9). Here, what is interpreted are data, not texts. Unstated in Moretti's account is the degree to which collecting such data itself requires a form of reading, not unlike a kind of mapping, which depends upon conventions and identifies particular details over others.

In the chapter on graphs, Moretti looks at the rise of the novel in several countries, noting that the number of novels published increases and then decreases at various times. By charting this data on a graph, where the number of novels published forms the y-axis and the years of publication form the x-axis, Moretti finds that patterns emerge. Moretti sees distinct cycles within the literary history, where other observers might be content to identify only individual cases. For example, noting rapid downturns in the publication of novels in England during the 1780s and again in the 1810s, Moretti concedes that the American Revolution and the Napoleonic wars may have contributed to these slumps, but he will argue that they are merely moments within "a recurring pattern of ups and downs" (2005: 13). His identification of literary historical cycles leads him back to the concept of genre, which he now understands as "the morphological embodiment" of cycles (17). Yet this too is a form of mapping, as Moretti plots what appears to be geographical data on his charts. At this point, however, he is no longer working directly with texts, but with data sets within which, it is to be assumed, individual texts are lodged. In this model, only broad tendencies in literary history can be identified, and the specific texts are not interpreted or even read. However, in order to determine the narrative form or genre of the texts which make up the data, someone, somewhere must be discerning and establishing the morphological characteristics of these literary works; that is, reading is still required.

MAPPING THE TEXT

In the section of *Graphs, Maps, Trees* devoted to maps, Moretti does offer a method of approaching texts that involves reading, although mapping the text for Moretti will not require close reading, and certainly not close reading of the sort that treats the text as an autonomous formal unit in the ways that the American "New Criticism" or the English "practical criticism" did. The process is more like extracting bits of information, transferring such bits onto a spatial diagram, and then interpreting the resulting diagram. This clearly requires that one read the original text, if only to find those elements that will form the points on the map, but Moretti insists that this does not involve interpreting the literary text as a freestanding formal entity in itself. Indeed, as we have observed, Moretti eschews any consideration of interpretive criticism in favour of explanation. Moretti sums up the function of the "literary map" in the following way:

> You choose a unit—walks, lawsuits, luxury goods, whatever—find its occurrences, place them in space ... or in other words: you *reduce* the text to a few elements, and *abstract* them from the narrative flow, and construct a new, *artificial* object like the maps I have been discussing. And with a little luck, these maps will be *more than the sum of their parts*: they will possess "emerging" qualities, which were not visible at the lower level.
>
> (2005: 53, ellipsis in original)

Moretti's tongue-in-check reference to "a little luck" might be said to belie the scientific pretensions of the project, but it is clear that the game he is playing with geographic, or geometric, information in these narratives is intended to yield new, hitherto unforeseen, literary historical insights. Moretti adds that the literary map may not, by itself, explain anything significant about the text, but it "offers a model of the narrative universe which rearranges its components in a non-trivial way, and may bring some hidden patterns to the surface" (53–54).

Moretti focuses on "village stories," a popular genre in early nineteenth-century Britain and elsewhere, in order to demonstrate his argument. Examining Mary Mitford's *Our Village* (1824), he leaves aside for the moment the actual geography of the place (i.e. Three Mile Cross, in Berkshire, "a dozen miles south of Reading"), and instead plots his own diagram in which key events or persons in each of the twenty-four stories are figured as points. The village itself is the centre, and the elements from various stories seem to form concentric circles, radiating outward from the village. A typical episode in these stories, Moretti notes, is the "country walk," in which the narrator leaves the village, reaches a destination, and returns home. As these walks go in a different direction each time, a diagram of the walks tend to reveal a concentric pattern. This pattern represents the essential chronotope, to use Mikhail Bakhtin's term, of the village story, a feature, Moretti insists, that is not exclusive to Mitford's story but is found in all village stories.

It is important to recall that the map does not in itself explain the phenomenon, rather, it helps to identify a phenomenon that then needs to be explained. Moretti understands the geography of rural life to be circular and, citing John Barrell's *The Idea of Landscape and the Sense of Place, 1730–1840*, he notes that rural villagers in an "open-field parish" would have experienced geography, the space of the place, differently from those who were merely visiting or passing through. The villager who rarely, if ever, left the parish would naturally see the parish as the centre, and envision the geography of the place accordingly, whereas the traveller passing through would have a mental image that was linear by comparison. Moreover, the daily life of the rustic is depicted as leisurely, with slow strolls and picturesque views of nature, and Moretti points out that, "for each page devoted to agricultural labor, there must be twenty on flowers and trees" (2005: 39). Undoubtedly, part of the appeal of the village story is that it offers urban readers a glimpse of a simpler, more "natural" life; casual observation of nature represents a pleasurable leisure activity, like reading itself, but the geographical figure of circles, as opposed to lines, locates the observer in a freer space. The linear grid of urban experience is replaced, for the reader, by the circular rings of country life.

Indeed, by turning to other village stories and "mapping" them in a similar way, Moretti develops a graphic history of modernization through the changing geography of the village space. In England, the acts of enclosure, beginning in the early sixteenth century, and intensifying by means of acts of Parliament in subsequent centuries, effectively imposed a grid or linear geography on what were open or "common" spaces. But even where it was not so formalized, it is possible to see a kind of grid-map emerging, with highways and later, railways, carving up the rustic space and a more urban model of living imposed on the landscape. One might call this, after Gilles Deleuze's distinction, the striation of smooth space (see, e.g., Deleuze and Guattari 1987: 479). Much of this is observable in actual maps produced before and after these modernizing events. Moretti argues that one can actually "see" this process using the maps created by reading these stories over many years. The breakdown of the symbolic space of the village is reflected in the breakdown of the literary chronotope itself, and the village becomes part of the broader region or the nation. Later editions of Mitford's *Our Village* show fewer country strolls, wider circles extending farther from the village centre, even beyond the borders of Berkshire. By the 1832 edition, as Moretti puts it, "the village's centripetal force is reduced to nothing, and the bulk of the book moves away, thirty miles, sixty, more, to play dumb parlour games in the mansions of the elite (and, again, ever more frequently in the past)" (2005: 59).

Moretti's own parlour game, his decision to plot the location of the various tales in *Our Village* in a diagram loosely linked to a map of the region in England, ends up revealing a phenomenon widely known in nineteenth-century literary studies. The canonical version is recounted in Williams's *The Country and the City*, as discussed earlier. But in *Atlas of the European Novel, 1800–1900*, Moretti had used a similar technique to show how maps "bring to light the *internal* logic of narrative: the semiotic domain around which a plot coalesces and self-organizes" (1998: 5). Although his use of diagrams was not exactly the same as in *Graphs, Maps, Trees*, Moretti uses maps to read nineteenth-century novels, revealing patterns he had not seen before. There he tries to plot the elements of the narrative on actual maps as a way to understand the spatial practices in novels.

In addition to offering a new way of reading individual texts or of practising literary history, Moretti presents a new approach to the corpus of literature. Although his literary geography is not really a model for how spatially oriented readers can explore the literary cartographies produced in narratives, it does offer an example of a sort of spatial approach to literature and literary history. A geocriticism, which would involve a critical theory and practice of spatiality in literature, could deploy the insights of Moretti's new "science" of literary history and of mapping. In the next chapter I will discuss a number of theorists and critics who challenge and extend thinking about the relations among space, place, mapping, and literary and social theory.

4

GEOCRITICISM

As I discussed in Chapter 1, the spatial turn in literary and cultural studies has occasioned a remarkable expansion in the number and quality of critical works on space, place, and mapping with respect to literature, and this has been most evident in the transdisciplinary field known as "theory." It is not merely that matters of space, place, and mapping have increasingly informed the research of literary and cultural theorists, but also that theory is itself a crucial domain of spatiality studies. As David Harvey has argued,

> [b]eneath the veneer of common-sense and seemingly "natural" ideas about space and time, there lie hidden terrains of ambiguity, contradiction, and struggle. Conflicts arise not merely out of admittedly diverse subjective appreciations, but because different objective material qualities of time and space are deemed relevant to social life in different situations. Important battles likewise occur in the realms of scientific, social, and aesthetic theory, as well as in practice. How we represent space and time in theory matters, because it affects how we and others interpret and then act with respect to the world.
>
> (Harvey 1990: 205)

In this chapter I would like to discuss several important theorists whose enhanced attention to matters of spatiality has distinguished their own work and made them particularly influential in literary and cultural studies. For the most part, all of these theorists have had to overcome, to a greater or lesser extent, the older bias against spatiality in favour of temporality. As Michel Foucault suggested, the earlier discourse of nineteenth-century philosophy was dominated by concepts of time, history, evolution, linear progress and teleology. In the twentieth century, there were those who maintained, as Foucault recounts with regard to a particularly pointed critic of his "Of Other Spaces" lecture, "that *space* was reactionary and capitalist, but *history* and *becoming* are revolutionary" (1982: 252). However, and, thanks in part to the variety and pertinence of spatial theories and practices, Foucault goes on to argue that such a view would now be laughable. One term that encompasses this variety of theories and practices which have motivated the spatial turn in literary and cultural studies is *geocriticism*.

Although the theory of geocriticism as elaborated by Bertrand Westphal in his book of that title is an important contribution to spatiality studies, which I will discuss in more detail later, I understand geocriticism more broadly, and I include under its auspices the variety of other critics and thinkers that will be examined in this chapter. The poetics and production of space, along with the spatial analytics of power and the examination of gender and spatiality, seem to me especially relevant, as does spatial philosophy and criticism. In speaking of Foucault's work, I have also used the term *cartographics*, which (like semiotics or technics or Louis Marin's "utopics") probably sounds more technical than it should, to designate a set of critical practices that seek to engage with the issues of spatial relations in connection with cultural and social theory. And this would include literary and artistic endeavours. Geocriticism or spatial critical theory, then, is broadly understood to include both aesthetics and politics, as elements in a constellation of interdisciplinary methods designed to gain a comprehensive and nuanced understanding of the ever-changing spatial relations that determine our current, postmodern, world. These practices are not immune to the transformative forces that have so radically affected the natural and social sciences in recent years. Geocriticism situates mapping and spatial analysis firmly within the framework of those other fields of study, while remaining pliable enough to fit instances that are not properly situated in the domain of geographic inquiry traditionally conceived, such as literature itself.

It seems to me that a fundamental task for geocriticism is to analyse, explore, and theorize these new cartographies that aid us in making sense of our places and spaces in the world. Geocriticism would have to take into account the ways in which spatial practices—including, of course, geographical mapping itself, but also such productions of knowledge as ethnography or economics—are employed and deployed, both for repressive ends and as means to aid political liberation. As a way to analyse literary texts, but also as an approach to social criticism, geocriticism can perhaps uncover hidden relations of power in those other spaces that a critical theory less attuned to spatiality might well overlook.

A POETICS OF SPACE

Gaston Bachelard (1884–1962) was a French philosopher of science whose influential work later informed the thinking of Louis Althusser, Michel Foucault, Jacques Derrida, and others. In *The Poetics of Space* (1969, originally published in French in 1958), Bachelard engages in a phenomenological investigation of the spaces of everyday life, focusing attention especially on the domestic sphere, with its attendant spaces and objects, such as its rooms, the cellar, the attic, the corners, as well as the furniture. Bachelard's chief concern is with the *poetic image*, and part of his analysis has to do with the epistemological question of how readers can grasp the poetic image in its reality when it would seem that only the poet has access to the actual experience of the image. As Bachelard puts it, "the reader of poems is asked to consider an image not as an object and even less as the substitute for an object, but to seize its specific reality" (1969: xv). He asserts that rationality or psychology cannot really explain the apprehension of the poetic image that requires to be understood more in terms of the daydream, a visceral, nearly pre-cognitive experience that may be explored through phenomenology.

Unlike many of the other theorists discussed in this chapter and throughout this book, Bachelard's primary interest is not in what Barbara Piatti has called *geospace* (2008: 22–23), the "real" spaces of geography, but with poetic space or the space of the imagination. Of course, this is not to say that Bachelard ignores "real" spaces. The domestic spaces of a house, as well as the homely images of a nest or shell, do refer to actual spaces inhabited by a body, after all. It is just that Bachelard's *topophilic* orientation, as he calls it, limits him to those "spaces we love," to "quite simple images of *felicitous space*" (xxxi). As such, even where he focuses on the real spaces within a house, such as the cellar or the wardrobe, he is always most interested in the individual subject's imaginative response to the experience of those spaces. Attached to the domestic space's protective value, which can be a positive one, are also imagined values, "which soon become dominant" (xxxi–xxxii). Bachelard continues,

> Space that has been seized upon by the imagination cannot remain indifferent space subject to the measures and estimates of the surveyor. It has been lived in, not in its positivity, but with all the partiality of the imagination. Particularly, it nearly always exercises an attraction. For it concentrates being within limits that protect. In the realm of images, the play between the exterior and intimacy is not a balanced one. ... But images do not adapt themselves very well to quiet ideas, or above all, to definitive ideas. The imagination is ceaselessly imagining and enriching itself with new images.
>
> (1969: xxxii)

Bachelard begins with the house or home, which, when broadly conceived, is the fundamental space of the human imagination: "all really inhabited space bears the essence of the notion of home" (1969: 5). He points out that the imagination may turn even shadows into "walls" of shelter, and in discussing "the poetic depth of the space of the house," Bachelard maintains that "the chief benefit of the house" is that "the house shelters day-dreaming, the house protects the dreamer, the house allows one to dream in peace" (6). Given the significance that he attaches to reverie, memory, and space for the individual psychological subject, Bachelard suggests **topoanalysis** as a necessary supplement to psychoanalysis (8). In such places, "a great many of our memories are housed" and "all our lives we come back to them in daydreams" (8). Hence, the experience of time is actually frozen in discrete moments in our memory, photographic or spatial arrangements, such that space assumes a greater importance than a temporality that is no longer understood in terms of a fluvial metaphor. In his assessment of Bachelard's argument, David Harvey concludes, "if it is true that time is always memorialized not as flow, but as memories of experienced places and spaces, then history must indeed give way to poetry, time to space, as the fundamental material of social expression" (1990: 218).

Bachelard's *Poetics of Space* deals with the interior spaces of the mind and the imagination, and therefore the poetics is less attuned to the geographic or cartographic projects taken up by other spatially oriented critics. Nevertheless, his exploration of the inner spaces of the imagination continues to exert influence over writers, whose work ventures far beyond the simple pleasures of the well-furnished domicile.

THE PRODUCTION OF SPACE

One of the most influential works of spatial theory, itself at once both a reflection of and a motive force in the spatial turn, is *The Production of Space* (1991; originally published in 1974) by the French Marxist philosopher and social critic Henri Lefebvre (1901–1991). It is a difficult book, performing more than explaining a sort of "spatial dialectic," as it distinguishes between abstract space and social space. Nevertheless, Lefebvre's arguments have helped to inform the critical social theories of David Harvey and Edward Soja, and *The Production of Space*, whether cited by name or not, has had wide-ranging effects in geography, urban studies, architecture, and sociology, as well as in philosophy, literature, and cultural studies. Indeed, Soja has called *The Production of Space* "arguably the most important book ever written about the social and historical significance of human spatiality and the particular powers of the spatial imagination" (1996: 8).

Lefebvre's astonishingly bold thesis is already announced in the title. Space, here meaning social space, is not the empty container of Cartesian or Kantian thought, but a social product made possible by human effort. From the initial proposition, "that (social) space is a (social) product" (1991: 30), Lefebvre presents a careful and broadly conceived exposition of the production of space; as he explains,

> Space is not produced in the sense that a kilogram of sugar or a yard of cloth is produced. Nor is it an aggregate of the places or locations of such products as sugar, wheat or cloth. Does it then come into being after the fashion of the superstructure? Again, no. It would be more accurate to say that it is at once a precondition and a result of social superstructures. The **state** and each of its constituent institutions call for spaces—but spaces which they can then organize according to their specific requirements; so there is no sense in which space can be treated solely as an *a priori* condition of these institutions and the state which presides over them. Is space a social relationship? Certainly—but one which is inherent to property relationships (especially the ownership of the earth, of land) and also closely bound up with the forces of production (which impose a form on that earth or land); here we see the polyvalence of social space, its "reality" at once formal and material. Though a *product* to be used, to be consumed, it is also a *means of production*; networks of exchange and flows of raw materials and energy fashion space and are determined by it. Thus the means of production, produced as such, cannot be separated either from the social division of labour which shapes it, or from the state and the superstructures of society.
>
> (1991: 85)

It follows from this hypothesis that space is also deeply historical, grounded in the developing modes of production and susceptible to conflicting processes: "Every society—and hence every mode of production [...]—produces a space, its own space" (1991: 31).

As Phillip E. Wegner has observed, Lefebvre's theory is distinct from other spatially oriented theoretical traditions, such as structuralism or phenomenology, in that "space is itself never constituted as a singularity," but that it is polyvalent and constituted by a "dialectically interwoven matrix" of human interactions (Wegner 2002b: 182). Lefebvre establishes a "conceptual triad" related to the various ways in which we experience and represent social space. The three elements of this triad are *spatial practice*, *representations of space*, and *representational spaces*, and they correspond to three modes of being and apprehending space, respectively the domains of the *perceived*, the *conceived*, and the *lived* (Lefebvre 1991: 33–40). "The spatial practice of a society secretes that society's space," writes Lefebvre; "From the analytic standpoint, the spatial practice of a society is revealed through the deciphering of its space" (38). Representations of space, in this matrix, refer to "conceptualized space, the space of scientists, planners, urbanists, technocratic subdividers and social engineers, as of a certain type of artist with a scientific bent—all of whom identify what is lived and what is perceived with what is conceived" (38). This "conceived" space is closer to the characterization of space in traditional theories. Finally representational spaces refer to "space as directly *lived* through its associated images and symbols, and hence the space of 'inhabitants' and 'users' ... This is the dominated—and hence passively experienced—space which the imagination seeks to change and appropriate" (39).

In his lengthy analysis of the production of space, Lefebvre charts the increasing significance and eventual domination of the visual register (over those of the other senses) with the development of the capitalist mode of production and the emergence of an "abstract space." Abstract space appears, but only appears (although appearance is also its strength) *homogeneous*, but really homogeneity is "its goal, its orientation, its 'lens'" (287–88). With the predominance of the visual or geometric register of abstract space, both lived experience and perceptions of space become more fragmented, tentative, and incomplete. It is partly from this sense of the new organizations of space produced under a late-capitalist mode of production that induced Jameson to call for an aesthetic of cognitive mapping, which was discussed in the last chapter. Lefebvre's Marxist analysis also aligns well with (and of course was an influence upon) Harvey's theorization of time-space compression in the postmodern condition. Also, his open-ended investigations of spatiality in *The Production of Space* clearly form the foundation, albeit a rather fluid and protean one, for Soja's idea of "thirdspace," which combines aspects of the "real" and the "represented" spaces while also going beyond them: "Simultaneously real and imagined and more (both and also …), the exploration of Thirdspace can be described and inscribed to 'real-and-imagined' (or perhaps 'realandimagined'?) places" (Soja 1996: 11; ellipsis in original).

Lefebvre's analysis of the production of space has fascinating resonances with the investigations of power and knowledge being undertaken by Foucault at roughly the same time. Foucault's work had long been attentive to matters of spatiality, but his theory of power as he outlined it in his works of the 1970s has proved extremely influential on critical, social and literary theory.

SPACES OF POWER

Although his genealogical studies of the 1970s have become important to many critics and theorists engaged in spatiality studies, Foucault had already demonstrated in his earlier writings the significance of space and spatial relations. As I have already noted, in his brief lecture on heterotopia and the spaces of everyday life, first presented in 1967 (but not published until 1984 as "Des espaces autres"), he observed that the present moment represented "the epoch of space" (1986: 22). Foucault was speaking, at least in part, to the then contemporary debates between structuralists and phenomenologists, among others, but the crucial insight that the historical moment had come to be dominated by spatial rather than, or in addition to, temporal considerations now appears to be almost a commonplace. The spatial turn in the humanities and social sciences owes much of its force to the prevailing sense that space is not merely a backdrop or setting for events, an empty container to be filled with actions or movements, or something to be treated as "the dead, the fixed, the undialectical, the immobile" (Foucault

1980b: 70). Rather, space was both a product and productive, as Lefebvre made abundantly clear in *The Production of Space*; as Foucault went on to suggest, it produces us, in fact. Indeed, Foucault's spatial analysis of power, which underlies his entire multifaceted and diverse body of work, places us in a better position today, after the spatial turn, to recognize the importance of space to our critiques of literature, society, and culture.

As has frequently been pointed out, by admirers and detractors alike, Foucault's historical analysis of power and knowledge draws heavily upon a discourse of spatiality, which appears only sometimes metaphorically, as in his use of the phrase, "carcerel archipelago," in *Discipline and Punish* (1977; originally 1975), and at others quite literally, as in his careful discussion of panopticism in the same book. In his earliest "archaeologies" of madness, sickness, and the human sciences more generally, Foucault employed methods that uncovered the layers of sedimented knowledge in order to pinpoint the "birth" of the asylum, the clinic, or the human sciences at large. He identified the spatial significance of the order of things, both in a geographical sense, such as the movement from exile to enclosure as public responses to appearance of contagious diseases in a population, and in a more abstract sense, as with the collection and organization of data into charts or tables. Later, with his genealogical researches into the disciplinary formations of individuality and the history of sexuality, he mapped the mobile circuitry of power relations in a distinctly spatial array, even as the trajectory of his historical narrative enfolded the spaces upon each other. Deleuze, in his review of *Discipline and Punish*, famously named Foucault a "new cartographer," one who maps social forces organized into diagrams, which Deleuze claims is "a map, or several super-imposed maps" (Deleuze 1988: 44). Foucault's spatial analysis of power and knowledge in modern social formations forms part of a larger project or even methodology that might be labeled *cartographics*, as I have suggested (see Tally 1996: 414). Not unlike Edward Soja's "trialectics" or Louis Marin's "utopics," cartographics, as part of the Foucauldian inquiry into the relations of power in modern societies, makes possible a careful, meticulous analysis of the mappings within, and of, those societies. Foucault's cartography of power is an important resource for understanding the ways in which this cartographic imperative both emerges and continues to exert its subtle, but pervasive, force.

In "Of Other Spaces," Foucault distinguishes the interior spaces analysed by Bachelard in *The Poetics of Space*, among others, from the exterior space [*l'espace du dehors*] in which we live, and which constitutes our life, our time, and our history. As Foucault puts it, "this space that gnaws and claws at us" is a heterogeneous space (1986: 23). His cartographies of power, his patient yet thrilling analysis of this heterogeneous space that forms individuals and groups as subjects while also representing the fluid milieus through which social forces move, emerge from his engagement with specific social institutions, notably the mental asylum, the clinic, and the prison; however, these local analyses quickly expand into a broader social sphere where the spatial relations of power become visible throughout the social body, and such spatial relations affect the determination of both "the normal" and "the pathological" (to utilize the title of the book by Foucault's predecessor Georges Canguillem [1991]) in innumerable, often unseen, ways.

In his so-called archaeological and genealogical works of the 1960s and 1970s, Foucault meticulously researched and analyzed the ways in which modern social formations have emerged. In the course of several important studies, he explored how the general character of modern societies, as well as the social processes that organize, structure, and condition the minutest aspects of everyday life within those societies, disclose an increasingly prominent and highly nuanced process of spatialization. As Foucault's work demonstrates, this spatialization appears not only with respect to phenomena traditionally associated with geography or geographic knowledge, but also in such related (or not so visibly related) fields as demography, medicine, urban and regional planning, and education, not to mention the burgeoning social sciences that began to emerge in the nineteenth century, such as psychology, sociology, ethnography and economics. From his *History of Madness* (first published as *Folie et Déraison: Histoire de la folie à l'âge classique* in 1961) to his three *History of Sexuality* volumes of the late 1970s and early 1980s, Foucault investigated the processes by which bodies become situated, distributed, classified, regulated, and identified in mobile and changing spatial matrices. The archaeology or genealogy of the modern world, the "history of the present" as he called it in *Discipline and Punish* (1977: 31), reveals a densely stratified but thoroughly flexible and mutable arrangement of spaces.

Although the two thinkers approach the spatiality of modern, or postmodern, societies from entirely different perspectives, Foucault's work has fascinating resonances with Jameson's briefly sketched history of spatial formations in *Postmodernism, or, the Cultural Logic of Late Capitalism* (1991), which I discussed at the end of the last chapter. Drawing upon Lefebvre's theorization of the production of space, Jameson outlines the manner in which each successive mode of production, and more particularly, each stage of development within the capitalist mode of production, has "generated a type of space unique to it." For Jameson's Marxist analysis these types of space "are all the result of a discontinuous expansion of quantum leaps in the enlargement of capital" (1991: 410). Like Foucault, Jameson finds that the organization of social space is subject to discontinuous changes or ruptures, which then call for new ways of mapping. Unlike Foucault, however, Jameson's understanding of these shifting social and spatial forms is rooted in the material processes and functions of capital itself, rather than in what Jameson somewhat dismissively refers to as "that shadowy and mythical entity Foucault called 'power'" (410), a complaint that Lefebvre would likely share. Jameson understands capital itself to be the motive force behind spatial and political order, and the nearly unrepresentable space in which we find ourselves situated at any given moment must be grasped in connection with such vital economic relations as labour, wages, monetary policies and financialization. Foucault's cartography of power is not absolutely inconsistent with the historical mapping of the production of space in Lefebvre or Jameson, but his methods and goals are quite different. Nevertheless, his depiction of spatial organization and reorganization through relations of "power/knowledge" does present points of intersection with the Marxist critique, as can be seen in the important work of Marxist geographers such as Harvey, Soja, and Derek Gregory (see 1994), all of whom derive inspiration from Lefebvre, Jameson, and Foucault.

Foucault's theory of power as pervasive, capillary, and productive, hardly presents power as immaterial, and one might argue that capital, or the power relations mobilized and maintained by the conditions made possible by a specifically capitalist mode of production, is still a part of Foucault's *diagram*, as Deleuze termed it in his review of *Discipline and Punish* (Deleuze 1988: 23–24). What Deleuze designates as a diagram in Foucault could be compared with Jameson's notion of a cognitive mapping. Especially in his famous chapter on panopticism and on Jeremy Bentham's *Panopticon*, Foucault discusses the emergence of an increasingly spatialized organization of social forces, and this enhanced spatialization is a critical and defining aspect of the modern (and postmodern) condition. This spatialization of social forces appears not only in a kind of direct geographical boundary-drawing or geographical demarcation, as in the "strict spatial partitioning" used to combat an outbreak of the bubonic plague (Foucault 1977: 195), but also in the more general ordering of demographic, economic, political, and medical data, as elaborated in *The Birth of the Clinic* (1963). A crucial feature of Foucault's vision of the characteristically modern society is the scientific distribution and codification of individuals in space. Hence, the surplus significance give to *le regard* or "the gaze" in these books, broadly conceived as including not only direct observation but also the collecting and ordering of information by which structures of power/knowledge help to create the modern individual, offers a practical model of the spatial distribution. The eye of power operates automatically, and eventually its effectiveness lies not so much in surveillance by others as in that more pervasive and subtle self-regulation that Friedrich Nietzsche had already identified with the feeling of bad conscience in *The Genealogy of Morals*. From his early archaeologies of knowledge in the books on the emergence of the asylum and the clinic to his genealogies of power and the emergence of the subject in the books on prisons and sexuality, Foucault demonstrates the profound spatialization of social organization and experience.

As early as his *History of Madness* (first published in 1961), Foucault had described the emergence of the society administered in terms of the organization and registration of individuals in a spatialized matrix. In this work, Foucault examines techniques for identifying, classifying, and treating madness, culminating in the emergence of the modern mental asylum. The birth of the asylum, from the premodern ostracization of madmen from town limits and the haunting image of the medieval Ship of Fools (*Das Narrenschiff*) to what Foucault calls "the great confinement," is part of a powerful and nuanced centralization, classification, and organization of space. This involved the power to categorize individuals, to place them in certain recognizable groups, and to locate them in suitable places; that is, "the insane" become a special subset of the general population, not to be excluded but to be rigorously included. This process also entailed the physical placement of such individuals in a particular location, a hospital or asylum where they would not simply be isolated from others, but studied, treated, and cured. Although Foucault does not argue for a formal or causal link between the two developments, he does observe that the great confinement is contemporaneous with technological and cultural transformations in the capitalist mode of production. For example, the early asylum housed not only the mentally ill, but the poor and the "idle" as well. In fact, before and during the eighteenth century, the distinction may not always have seemed clear, since idleness was regarded as a sign of moral and mental infirmity. Later, the need for a "reserve army of surplus labor," as Karl Marx would call the unemployed, gave social value to the pauper, who now needed to be distinguished from the insane (see Foucault 1965: 218–19). As the methods for classifying and situating disparate individuals became more refined, so the organization of social space gained precedence over other areas of everyday life. This is also the point at which Foucault identifies the increasing urbanization of French society, such that, in France, urban planning, police surveillance, and actual mapping begin to take on the form of models for the new national social organization as a whole.

In his next book, *The Birth of the Clinic* (1963; translated into English in 1973), Foucault started to move away from centralization as the model for the spatialization of power and knowledge, and he began to outline the ways in which spatial practices become more fluid, flexible, and resilient. Although he was still some distance from his later formulation of a theory of power, in which power is characterized by its capillary and decentralized nature, he shows in this text how the "medical gaze" operates in a far more subtle and widespread manner than one might normally think; rather than emerging as the result of centripetal forces to centralize medicine, the medical gaze radiates throughout the social body. To be sure, medical practices and the knowledge to be gained through them in the nineteenth century have undoubtedly become more centralized in the form of the state regulation and a bio-political power/knowledge complex, but here Foucault indicates the degree to which the spatial organization of individuals in society had less to do with confinement and more to do with distribution. Under the regime of the healthy society, individuals were subject to increased regulation and registration, located in identifiable places, monitored, and catalogued, but without their necessarily being sequestered in a particular location. As Foucault later put it in an interview,

> Doctors at that time were among other things the specialists of space. They posed four fundamental problems. That of local conditions (regional climates, soil, humidity or dryness ...); that of co-existences (either between men, questions of density and proximity, or between men and things, the question of water, sewage, ventilation, or between men and animals, the question of stables and abattoirs, or between men and the dead, the question of cemeteries); that of residences (the environment, urban problems); that of displacements (the migration of men, the propagation of diseases). Doctors were, along with the military, the first managers of collective space.
>
> (1980a: 150–51)

From here, the gaze was no longer limited to a particular place in which it operated, but it became generalized to cover the whole social field: "if the intervention of the doctors was of capital importance in this period, this was because it was demanded by a whole new range of political and economic problems" (1980a: 151). In this view of the effective functioning of power and knowledge throughout the spatio-political domain, Foucault's "archaeology of the medical gaze" (the book's original subtitle) points to his later account of genealogy of disciplinary practices in *Discipline and Punish*.

Perhaps the most famous chapter of *Discipline and Punish*, "Panopticism" also makes the case most clearly for an intensely spatial organization of social relations. The chapter opens with a description of ways in which a city stricken with the black plague was to be organized, and it thus recalls the arguments regarding the treatment of madness and physical illness as chronicled in the earlier studies. Strict spatial partitioning, constant surveillance, the distribution and localization of individuals, constant monitoring and registration of data, and an intensification and diffusion of the exercise of power, typified the social organization of the plague stricken town.

> This enclosed, segmented space, observed at every point, in which the individuals are inserted in a fixed place, in which the slightest movements are supervised, in which all events are recorded, in which an uninterrupted work of writing links the centre and the periphery, in which power is exercised without division, according to a continuous hierarchical figure, in which each individual is constantly located, examined and distributed among the living beings, the sick and the dead—all this constitutes a compact model of disciplinary mechanism.

Foucault concludes this passage with the claim that, "this is the utopia of the perfectly governed city" (1977: 198).

Foucault takes this model in its instrumentality and effects to be identical to that described in Jeremy Bentham's 1791 *Panopticon*, a model prison and architectural apparatus in which those inside are subjected to continual surveillance; the subjects of the panopticon's machinery are permanently aware of being located within a well regulated, well monitored, social matrix. Even more than in his earlier studies, Foucault here takes spatial relations to be fundamental to the organization of the social field through the functioning of power and knowledge. As he explains, the Panopticon

> is polyvalent in its applications; it serves to reform prisoners, but also to treat patients, to instruct schoolchildren, to confine the insane, to supervise workers, to put beggars and idlers to work. It is a type of location of bodies in space, of distribution of individuals in relation to one another, of hierarchical organization, of disposition of centres and channels of power, of definition of the instruments and modes of intervention of power, which can be implemented in hospitals, workshops, schools, prisons. Whenever one is dealing with a multiplicity of individuals on whom a task or a particular form of behaviour must be imposed, the panoptic schema may be used.
>
> (1977: 205)

Foucault concludes with the rhetorical question: "Is it surprising that prisons resemble factories, schools, barracks, hospitals, which all resemble prisons?" (228).

In his study of Foucault's philosophy, Deleuze takes this to be the most important achievement of *Discipline and Punish*: isolating and describing the *diagram*, which is to say, map, of power. The generalization of the panoptic diagram beyond merely architectural applications in prisons or workhouses constitutes a new form of the social organization of space. As Deleuze understands it, "the diagram is no longer an auditory or visual archive, but a map, a cartography that is coextensive with the whole social field" (1988: 34). In disclosing this map of power, Foucault is himself a cartographer, mapping the spatial power-relations that actively produce, as well as minutely affect, the social domain. Unlike Jameson's and Lefebvre's conception of the production of space, Deleuze's Foucauldian analysis focuses not on capital as the organizing power, but on power itself, which presumably includes but is not limited to the economic mode of production. Or, as Deleuze summarizes his concept of the diagram in Foucault's analysis:

> We have seen that the relations between forces, or power relations, or microphysical, strategic, multipunctual and diffuse, that they

determined particular features and constituted pure functions. The diagram or abstract machine is the map of relations between forces, a map of density, or intensity, which proceeds by primary non-localizable relations ended every moment passes through every point, "or rather in relation from one point to another."

(1988: 36, translation modified; the last phrase is from Foucault 1978: 93)

While Deleuze's analysis here may seem abstract, his reading of Foucault's cartographic project reinforces the view of a social formation based upon the clear spatiality of relations of power.

THE LONG POEM OF WALKING

Michel de Certeau (1925–1986), in a fascinating rejoinder to Foucault's argument, contends that the street-level pedestrian, the window-shopper, or the *flâneur*, can both escape from the totalizing gaze of the eye of power, and can actively disrupt and reorganize the spatial relations of power. As I mentioned in Chapter 3, de Certeau examines the spatial practices of individuals or groups who are walking in the city, and he argues in *The Practice of Everyday Life* (1984) that these "spatial stories" can escape or undermine the force-fields of power that Foucault's exposition of panopticism reveals.

De Certeau begins his analysis of "walking in the city" by contrasting the perspective of the street-level walker with that of a "voyeur" who looks down upon the entire city from a lofty vantage. In what must now be read with a certain strange poignancy, the point of view de Certeau has in mind is that afforded from the observation deck of the World Trade Center; at the time of de Certeau's writing, New York's twin towers were the tallest skyscrapers in the world, and, situated at the far end of Manhattan, someone on top of the World Trade Center on a clear day could get an excellent view of the whole of Manhattan, as well as of other boroughs and parts of New Jersey across the Hudson River. De Certeau writes that "to be lifted to the summit of the World Trade Center is to be lifted out of the city's grasp" (1984: 92). From this aerie, "an Icarus flying above these waters," a person becomes a voyeur, able to "read" the city from a distance, "to be a solar Eye, looking down like a god. The exaltation of the scopic and gnostic drive: the fiction of knowledge is related to this lust to be a viewpoint and nothing more" (92). For de Certeau, the image of the city from this perspective is "the analogue of the facsimile produced ... by the space planner urbanist, city planner or cartographer" (92–93).

Conversely, de Certeau asserts that the "ordinary practitioners of the city" are down below, on the street: "they are walkers, *Wandersmänner*, whose bodies follow the thicks and thins of an urban 'text' they write without being able to read it" (93). Pointedly invoking Foucault's conclusions in *Discipline and Punish*, de Certeau argues that pedestrians attempt to locate "the practices that are foreign to the 'geometrical' or 'geographical' space of the visual, panoptic, or theoretical constructions" (93). He finds in the "speech acts" of pedestrians certain *spatial practices*: "these multiform, resistance, tricky and stubborn procedures that elude discipline" (96). Perhaps thinking of Baudelaire's, or Benjamin's, discussion of the *flâneur*, de Certeau identifies the pedestrian, the passer-by, the window-shopper, and the wanderer as the real authors of a city: "They are not localized; it is rather they that spatialize" (97).

The contrast of a panoptic overview that represents power/ knowledge and the relatively free and illegible movements of the street-level wanderer form the basis of what de Certeau calls "the long poem of walking." As he explains,

> The long poem of walking manipulates spatial organizations, no matter how panoptic they may be: it is neither foreign to them (it can take place only within them) not in conformity with them (it does not receive its identity from them). It creates shadows and ambiguities within them. It inserts its multitudinous references and citation into them (social models, cultural mores, personal factors). Within them it is itself the effect of successive encounters and occasions that constantly alter it and make it the other's blazon: in other words, it is like a peddler, carrying something surprising, transverse or attractive compared with the usual choice.
>
> (1984: 101)

As if to emphasize the difficulty or impossibility of positively localizing the *flâneur* in the geometric or panoptic space of a map, de Certeau says, "to walk is to lack a place" (103).

In a related discussion, de Certeau distinguishes between the itinerary and the map. As I mentioned in the last chapter, Jameson rightly noted that Kevin Lynch's "image of the city" had more to do with itineraries than with maps. In de Certeau's view, the difference is between "two poles of experience," between "either *seeing* (the knowledge of an order of places) and *going* (spatializing actions)" (1984: 119). The map is thus the totalizing and static overview of the solar Eye for de Certeau, whereas the itinerary or the tour, which is based not in descriptive overview by in narrative movement, makes possible transgression. The cartographer and city planner may establish a well ordered grid, but the pedestrian will find shortcuts or unmarked passages, becoming a "social delinquent" (129–30).

De Certeau's image of the itinerant pedestrian, "writing" the text of the city by moving through and within it, calls to mind Walter Benjamin's *Arcades Project*, discussed in the last chapter. In his assessment of Baudelaire, Benjamin recognizes that the gaze of the *flâneur*, in a sense, *rewrites* the story of the space, and in this way perhaps Benjamin prefigures de Certeau's concept of the pedestrian or passer-by as a social delinquent, fully possessed of agency, who can "manipulate spatial organizations." As Benjamin explains,

> For the first time, with Baudelaire, Paris becomes the subject of lyric poetry. This poetry is no hymn to the homeland; rather, the gaze of the allegorist, as it falls on the city, is the gaze of the alienated man. It is the gaze of the *flâneur*, whose way of life still conceals behind a mitigating nimbus the coming desolation of the big-city dweller. The *flâneur* still stands on the threshold ...
>
> (1999: 10)

The "gaze of the allegorist," at least from one point of view, can be seen as a counter-gaze to the panoptic organization of space, inasmuch as the allegorist by definition substitutes another story for the one presented. In a way, then, Benjamin's version of Baudelaire's *flâneur* offers another example of those spatial practices which resist the totalizing gaze from above, as de Certeau would have it. This is not, of course, to suggest that the pedestrian is inherently radical or politically progressive, only that the passer-by embodies and discloses alternatives to the seemingly omnipresent and ubiquitous spatializations of modern societies. In this, Foucault would almost certainly agree, for he recognized that various modes of resistance and redirections of power-relations are very much part of the constitution of the system as a whole.

Benjamin's idea of standing on the threshold, an image that recurs in much of his work, is itself a spatial as well as historical conception. In his writings, Benjamin frequently alludes to such figures, real or imaginary, as the threshold, the brink, the anteroom, the frontier, or the border, as if to emphasize the ambiguities of those liminal spaces. Referring to his own childhood and to "walking in the city" in "A Berlin Chronicle," he notes the fascination of "crossing the threshold" from one neighbourhood, and social class, to another: "this was a crossing of frontiers not only social but topographical, in the sense that whole networks of streets were opened up […]. But it is really a crossing, is it not, rather, an obstinate and voluptuous hovering on the brink, a hesitation that has its most cogent motive in the circumstance that beyond this frontier lies nothingness?" (1978: 11). Benjamin concludes this reflection by saying that "the places are countless in the great cities where one stands on the edge of the void" (11). Interestingly, in this passage from "A Berlin Chronicle" Benjamin compares the sensations of cross-ing into a poor neighbourhood with those mixed emotions, at once a yearning leavened with a sense of dread or anguish, with the experience of accosting a prostitute publicly. This fact reminds us that the social organization of spaces through the networks of power and knowledge (in Foucault), perhaps revised and resisted by the delinquent "street-walkers" (of de Certeau), and made all the more ambiguous by the urban *flâneur* (for

Benjamin), are also subject to analysis along the lines of sex and gender.

ENGENDERING SPACES

Among the foremost theorists of the spatial turn in social theory and cultural studies in recent decades have been feminist philosophers, geographers and critics. Perceiving that both the disciplinary field or profession of geography and the discourse of spatiality have frequently been male-dominated, feminist geographers like Gillian Rose (1962–) have argued that, as a consequence "geography holds a series of unstated assumptions about what men and women do, and that the discipline concentrates on the spaces, places, and landscapes that it sees as men's" (1993: 2). Feminist geography, along with feminist interventions in a number of other disciplines, aims to make visible the hitherto undisclosed gendering of spaces, while also establishing a revisionary critique of the power/knowledge relations of male-dominated social formations. In a sense, then, the feminist critique of geography calls for a new understanding of social space, on the grounds that such research reveals the "profound and intricate relations of space and the construction of a gendered reality" (Ganser 2009: 66).

In her important contribution to feminist geographical thinking, *Space, Place, and Gender* (1994), British geographer Doreen Massey (1944–) makes a compelling case for the idea that all spaces are inherently gendered. As she points out, "From the symbolic meaning of spaces/places and the clearly gendered messages which they transmit, to straightforward exclusion by violence, spaces and places are not only in themselves gendered but, in their being so, they both reflect and affect the ways in which gender is constructed and understood" (1994: 179). Although professional geographers have rarely discussed, or even acknowledged, the gendering of space, Massey reports that growing up in Manchester, England, it was intuitively apparent that there were certain public places that girls and women did not (and implicitly, perhaps, were not permitted to) go. Later, she noticed the very different effects that specific places had on men as opposed to women, such as the gallery of an art museum in which figures of nude women painted by men were on display. Massey notes that the list of examples could be multiplied considerably and she concludes:

> Space and place, spaces and places, and our senses of them (and such related things as our degrees of mobility) are gendered through and through. Moreover, they are gendered in a myriad different ways, which vary between cultures and over time. And this gendering of space and place both *reflects and has effects* back on the ways in which gender is constructed and understood in the societies in which we live.
>
> (1994: 185–86)

Massey contends that, by "taking gender seriously," geography would be better able to comprehend, and improve upon, sweeping changes in regional and urban planning, which required various assessments of the different constructions of gender in different regions, such as London versus the industrial northern England (1994: 189).

In some ways, the idea of gendered spaces appears a mere commonplace, since there are clearly certain spaces or types of place that are normally associated with women or men, something pointedly addressed in Virginia Woolf's *A Room of One's Own* (first published 1929). For instance, the notion that the home or the domestic sphere is a feminine space, or that the workplace or public sphere belongs to men, has long been understood if not always studied or theorized. In *Putting Women in Place: Feminist Geographers Make Sense of the World* (2001), the American geographers Mona Domosh and Joni Saeger both explore and call into question such common assumptions about everyday spaces. To take one example, they note, how in the Victorian era, dining rooms were frequently coded as masculine, partly because that was where fresh meat would be served on festive occasions thus associating the place with the pre-dominantly male sport of hunting; it was often decorated with painting of hunting scenes or with taxidermied trophies (2001: xix). Of course, some of these associations may be explained by this or that form of sexism or sexual discrimination, but Domosh and Saeger emphasize the degree to which the interrelations of space, place, and gender are complex and finely nuanced. In insisting that "space is gendered" (xxi), these geographers point to the often unacknowledged ways that the built environment is based on and actively shapes assumptions about gender roles in society.

In *Feminism and Geography* (1993), Rose explores "the masculinism of contemporary geographical discourse," by which the disciplinary field distinguishes and subordinates "the Other," here primarily understood as *the feminine* (9–10). Rose argues that two forms of masculinity condition and dominate the study of spaces and places: "Social-scientific masculinity asserts its authority by claiming access to a transparently real geographical world," which then "represses all reference to its Other in order to claim total knowledge," and "aesthetic masculinity ... establishes its power through claiming a heightened sensitivity to human experience," which enables this form to admit "the existence of its Other in order to establish a profundity of which it alone has the power to speak" (10–11). For Rose, such masculinized geographies prove to have severe limits to their epistemological value by either ignoring, or subordinating, the perspectives and influence of feminine and other apparently marginalized groups.

Although the critical force of Rose's study lies in the disclosure of the unquestioned and sometimes invisible assumptions of the geographical discourse she engages with, *Feminism and Geography* also points to strategies of resistance. For instance, she maintains that

> Feminist explorations of the different spaces of the contemporary city often reject the search for totality from a position of complete knowledge. Their work is more tentative, more grounded in the details of the everyday, and more likely to interpret social life and spaces in the city in terms of a radical heterogeneity.
>
> (1993: 133)

Rose then discusses "the possibility of a space which does not replicate the exclusions of the Same and the Other" (1993: 137), which she calls "paradoxical space." This involves a "sense of space which refuses to be a claim to territoriality and thus allows for radical difference" (150), and these "paradoxes" include a simultaneous occupation of the centre and the margin, as well as being within the Same/Other dichotomy but also elsewhere. It is by means of a "paradoxical geography" that feminism can imagine "a different kind of space through which difference is tolerated rather than erased" (155). Rose does not claim that paradoxical space is inherently liberatory, but she argues that the field of geography must acknowledge that "the grounds of its knowledge are unstable, shifting, uncertain and, above all, contested" (160).

Among these contested spaces are those in which movement or mobility, or the lack thereof, is most noticeable. In *A Road of Her Own* (2009), whose title is at once a play on and a critique of Woolf's *A Room of One's Own*, Alexandra Ganser criticizes the "masculinization of the road as a physical and social space," and she views "the literary representation of space as a gendered phenomenon" (66). In taking what has been perceived as a strictly male type of place as the emblem of a feminist literary sensibility, Ganser re-imagines the space and revises its customary mythic content, which takes its salient images from male writers such as Walt Whitman or Jack Kerouac, to include now the more ambiguous figures of the runaway, the kidnappee, and the sales-woman. Drawing in part upon the work of Rosi Braidotti, whose *Nomadic Subjects: Embodiment and Sexual Difference in Contemporary Feminist Theory* (2011) draws upon the writings of Deleuze, Ganser suggests that a "para-nomadism," a mobility "motivated by economic or political necessity (rather than wanderlust or adventurousness)" characterize a number of feminine road narra-tives, and that these alter the way one normally thinks of travel or "the road" (2009: 34–35). The **nomad** is not always a figure of emancipation, but nomadism can disrupt or alter the spatial organizations of a given geographical order.

NOMAD THOUGHT AND GEOPHILOSOPHY

The philosophical discourse of Gilles Deleuze (1925–1995) is permeated with explanatory images of spatiality, ranging from his persistent use of spatial terminology (e.g. diagram, plane, map, cartography, plateau, lines of flight, deterritorialization and reterritorialization, **smooth** and **striated** space) to his insistence that all thinking is necessarily tied to space, to territory, and to the earth. In his collaborative work with Félix Guattari and beyond, Deleuze developed a *nomadology*, during the same period that Lefebvre's ideas of the production of space and Foucault's spatial analytics of power emerged. Deleuze's "nomad thought" derives from his meticulous encounters with the history of philosophy, as well as his more politically incisive critiques of the organization of power and desire in Western civilization. From 1953 to 1968, Deleuze produced a number of studies on the works of individual philosophers (David Hume, Friedrich Nietzsche, Henri Bergson, Immanuel Kant, and Baruch Spinoza), and partly through his encounters with these thinkers he developed what he later called, borrowing the title of an essay on Nietzsche, "nomad thought." In major philosophical works, written in his "own voice" as he would later say, and also in his *Capitalism and Schizophrenia* volumes, *Anti-Oedipus* and *A Thousand Plateaus*, co-authored with Guattari (first published in 1972 and 1980 respectively), Deleuze would both characterize and demonstrate nomad thought.

In and through these philosophical explorations, Deleuze distinguishes between *nomads*, who are understood as such because of their border crossings or re-crossings, but also because of their conceptual demolition of the boundary lines themselves, and the *state* and "state philosophy," which are defined in terms of sedentary ordering, spatial measurement, the segmenting of the rank and file, and a conceptual gridding that attempts to assign stable places. In their occupation of space, their deconstruction of boundaries, and movement across surfaces, Deleuze's nomads continually map and remap, altering spaces even as they traverse them. They are in Deleuze's language, forces of deterritorialization, unsettling to a greater or lesser extent the metric ordering of space that is subject to the power of the state.

Although the chapter on "nomadology" appears in *A Thousand Plateaus* (1980; English translation, 1987), Deleuze had already made the distinction between nomad thought and state philosophy as early as 1968, in *Difference and Repetition* where he distinguishes between a "nomadic distribution" of the various components of Being in Spinoza's philosophy. He opposes Spinoza's conception of Being to the Cartesian theory of substances that, like the agricultural or statist model, distributes elements of Being by dividing them into fixed categories, demarcating territories and fencing them off from one another. He notes that the statist or Cartesian distribution of Being is rooted in the agricultural need to set proprietary boundaries and fix stable domains. Alternatively, there is "a completely other distribution, which must be called nomadic, a nomad *nomos*, without property, enclosure or measure," that does not involve "a division of that which is distributed but rather a division among those who distribute themselves in an open space—a space which is unlimited, or at least without precise limits" (Deleuze 1994: 36). He thus proposes that nomads have a qualitatively different kind of space from that of the state: "It is the difference between a *smooth* (vectoral, projective, topological) space and a *striated* (metric) space: in the first case 'space is occupied without being counted,' and in the second case 'space is counted in order to be occupied'" (Deleuze and Guattari 1987: 361–62).

For Deleuze and Guattari, the maritime model provides an example of this distinction, since "the sea is a smooth excellence, and yet it was the first to encounter the demands of increasingly strict striation" (479). Technological and artistic developments in cartographic techniques are partly responsible for such striations; for example, as we observed in Chapter 2 with respect to Jameson's "digression on cartography," the Mercator projection, which established and imposed upon the figured surface of the world a grid composed of parallels and meridians, is perhaps the most obvious striating strategy. The smooth space of the sea becomes a matrix upon which navigations between points along a Cartesian, *x*- and *y*-axis are charted. However, Deleuze's distinction of smooth and striated space cannot be taken as an anti-mapping position, nor should we think that he is opposed to the cognitive efforts to make sense of one's place or of the spatial relations constituting our world. Deleuze's nomad versus state spaces must not be confused with the simpler idea of liberated versus repressive spaces or even something like de Certeau's mobile pedestrians versus the eye of power gazing down from above. Indeed, as Deleuze and Guattari state, "smooth spaces are not in themselves liberatory. But the struggle is changed or displaced in them, and life reconstitutes its stakes, confronts new obstacles, invents new paces, switches adversaries. Never believe that smooth space will suffice to save us" (500).

In their introduction to *Deleuze and Space*, Ian Buchanan and Gregg Lambert explain how the analysis of the ways that smooth and striated space are assembled and mixed require Deleuze and Guattari to develop different modes of understanding such spaces. But notwithstanding these differences, the basic method is cartographic. As Buchanan and Lambert write, "This mapping of the different kinds of space that mix in each assemblage (social, political, but also geographical, biological, economic, aesthetic or musical, and so on) becomes the major task set out by the project they [Deleuze and Guattari] define as pragmatics or micro-politics" (2005: 5). Confronted with the crises of representation and with the emergence of the new spaces produced by late capitalism or postmodernity, Deleuze and Guattari "set out to develop a series of maps of these spaces in a pragmatic sense of finding 'a way through,' or a manner of orienting themselves (as they often say in the course of their analysis: 'now we are in a better position to draw a map'), which Kant earlier defined as the fundamental task of thinking as well" (Buchanan and Lambert 2005: 5–6).

Deleuze's nomadology and particularly his definition of smooth space offer a useful supplement to what is frequently (and, I believe, erroneously) viewed as Foucault's apparently total, Orwellian vision of the panoptic society and a carceral archipelago in which all of us are in the same position as the incarcerated prisoner of Bentham's infernal machine. Actually, Foucault's vision is no more, or less, totalizing than Deleuze's. It is true that Foucault does not admit the possibility of situating oneself "outside" power and power relations, but this is not the same thing as being permanently oppressed, since relations of power are protean and sometimes reversible. As Foucault makes explicitly clear in *The History of Sexuality, Volume I* (translated into

English 1978; originally published as *La Volonté de savoir* in 1976), power is productive, capillary, flowing through the social body, and not a property to be won or held. Undoubtedly, such "productive" power can, of course, produce unpleasant things, but it also produces us, our social relations, our knowledge and our experience. In this sense, to be situated within the mobile flow of forces in a society is also to be implicated in a spatial array, where near and far, high and low, centre and periphery, constitute our social being-in-the-world. From this perspective, power, like space, is not wielded, nor does it proceed in a uni-linear direction. Deleuze's nomads provide an apposite figure for a kind of resistance that is not exterior to relations of power, but exerts a force within their elaborate, mobile, and ever shifting web of spatial relations.

Deleuze is arguably the twentieth century's most spatial philosopher (see Buchanan and Lambert 2005), and, beyond his frequent deployment of spatial terms or his many spatial metaphors, he conceived philosophy as fundamentally spatial. In one of his final works, co-authored once again with Guattari and given the deceptively simple title of *What is Philosophy?* (1994), he lays out his case for a geophilosophy. The term *geophilosophy*, for Deleuze, refers less to a specialized subfield of philosophy than to a recognition in his view of the fundamentally spatial or geographical character of philosophy as a whole. As Deleuze and Guattari put it, "Subject and object give a poor approximation of thought. Thinking is neither a line drawn between subject and object nor a revolving of one around another. Rather, thinking takes place in the relationship of territory and the earth" (1994: 85).

In their useful guide to the subject, Mark Bonta and John Protevi characterize geophilosophy as Deleuze's (and Guattari's) "attempt to refound philosophy as materialist, earthly, and spatial. They seek to reorient philosophy from a concentration on temporality and historicity to spatiality and geography" (2004: 92). With geophilosophy, Deleuze reasserts the significance of spatiality for thought, and makes it a crucial category for philosophical reflection and concept-creation. In short, geo-philosophy joins with the poetics of space, the production of space, the spatial analytics of power and knowledge and the conception of sites and movements of resistance, in order to help form the theoretical bases of a geocriticism.

A GEOCENTRIC APPROACH

My use of the term *geocriticism*, in this chapter and elsewhere (see Tally 2011), does not follow from or coincide neatly with the work of the French literary critic Bertrand Westphal (1962–), but Westphal's geocritical approach to literary texts presents an intriguing method for examining the interrelations of space, place, and literature. In his programmatic and somewhat tentative study *Geocriticism: Real and Fictional Spaces* (2011), Westphal attempts to establish the background and the characteristics of this critical method, while also leaving geocriticism open to further critical elaboration and exploration. Drawing heavily upon the philosophy of Deleuze, the postmodern geographies of Harvey and Soja, as well as a host of novelists, other critics, scientists, and historians, Westphal argues that a proper study of literature must take into account the spatial and geographical fields, and that in the postmodern condition, the consideration of spatiality becomes an essential part any critical inquiry.

Westphal provides a theory and a method for analysing this interplay of spatial practices in literary texts, but his argument also draws on many disciplinary formations and cultural discourses, including architecture, urban studies, film, philosophy, sociology, postcolonial theory, gender studies, and, of course, geography and literary criticism. He insists that the geocritical approach must be resolutely interdisciplinary, and his own research demonstrates this commitment. However, as befits a literary theory, Westphal also acknowledges the degree to which geocriticism must take advantage of the specific effects that literary texts can provide. Referring to Soja's "third" space, that is, to the "real-and-imagined" space to which literature often opens a distinctive vista, he writes:

> In theory every space is situated at the crossroads of creative potential. We always return to literature and the mimetic arts in our

explorations, because, somewhere between reality and fiction, the one and the others know how to bring out the hidden potentialities of space-time without reducing them to stasis. The space-time revealed at the intersection of various mimetic representations is this third space that geocriticism proposes to explore. Geocriticism will work to map possible worlds, to create plural and paradoxical maps, because it embraces space in its mobile heterogeneity.

(2011: 73)

The wide-ranging argument befits the topic, as geocriticism seeks to explore the spaces of literature in multiple senses. Westphal initially outlines a landscape of theoretical positions, demonstrating how modernism and postmodernism have altered fundamentally the ways in which thinkers understand space, no longer as a stable or inert category but rather as a complex, heterogeneous phenomenon. This concept of space allows for a more dynamic or transgressive movement that literature explores in its frequently problematic representations of space, in which the lines between fictional and real spaces are constantly crossed and re-crossed. Westphal maintains that these three broad categories: spatiotemporality, transgressivity, and referentiality, are the foundations of geocritical practice.

Although he allows his geocriticism to be defined broadly, in order to include a number of spatially oriented critical practices, Westphal's own most distinctive contribution appears to be the particular "geocentric" or "geocentred" approach that he espouses. He argues that the geocritic ought to eschew the traditional ego-centred approach to literature and space, and focus instead on the geographical locus itself. For example, instead of looking at the ways in which Dickens represents London in his novels, Westphal's geocritic starts with London (or, perhaps, just a small portion of it, given the enormity both of the actual metropolis and of the manifold literary representations of it), and then proceed to look at various texts which attempt to represent it. He insists that "Unlike most literary approaches to space ... geocriticism tends to favor a geocentered approach" (112). This means establishing in advance a particular place to be studied, such as a neighbourhood, a city, a region, or even a country, and then gathering and reading texts that in some way represent it. For example, in his own research, Westphal and his collaborators have produced a study of "the Mediterranean" using such a geocentric approach, and he has also written a study of the representations of Zanzibar in tourist brochures. In this way, a sort of literary geography of a place can be established through the accumulation and analysis of a broad, interdisciplinary corpus of texts.

In his methodological discussion of geocriticism, Westphal identifies four elements that the geocritic must keep in mind (2011: 111–47). First, adhering to the principle of *multifocalization*, the geocritic is required to engage with many different points of view on the grounds that a variety of perspectives are necessary to establish the contours of literary space and to ensure that its representation is not limited by individual bias or stereotyping. Second, the geocritic is required to embrace *polysensoriality*, inasmuch as the space under consideration may not be perceived by vision alone, but also by smell, or sound; as Paul Rodaway has pointed out in his *Sensuous Geographies* (1994), although the visual register dominates geography, the other senses are almost as important as sources of the meanings humans attach to and associate with places. Third, Westphal argues that geocritics must maintain a *stratigraphic vision*, in which the *topos* is understood to comprise multiple layers of meaning, deterritorialized and reterritorialized; attention to surface alone would not be sufficient to understand the place, for as Lefebvre notes in *The Production of Space*, social space "emerged in all its diversity ... with a structure far more reminiscent of a *mille-feuille* pastry than of the homogeneous and isotorphic space of classical (Euclidean/Cartesian) mathematics" (1991: 86). Finally, geocritics must keep *intertextuality* to the fore in their research, noting that all textual spaces necessarily encompass, "interface" with, or relate in other ways to other spaces in literature and in reality. Westphal's geocritical approach thus attempts to pry criticism loose from an egocentrism, with respect to either the writer or the reader, and opens literary studies to a polyvalent interaction of spatial and discursive practices.

In Westphal's effort to eschew the potential bias of the individual author's egocentric approach to a given place, he risks another form of egocentrism in invoking the perspective of the geocritical researcher. For example, who decides which texts to include in the corpus of literature that will be used to "read" a place? Even if it is formed through collaborative or collective efforts, the points of view of the individual researchers are implicated in the overall phenomenology of the place. Westphal's multifocal position is that the more perspectives admitted, the more likely one is to achieve a diverse, well-rounded and possibly unbiased image of the spaces and places involved. However, as a cognitive matter, in the sense that geocriticism can be used to understand a place, Westphal's geocentred approach does not wholly escape the problem of the subject.

It should be clear from this characterization that the work Westphal envisions is likely to involve broadly collaborative or quasi-scientific research, not unlike Franco Moretti's "distant reading" project which I discussed in the last chapter. Any meaningful corpus of texts that aim to represent a given place, like Moretti's attempt to understand the novel as a form in its millions of individual instances, will require far more material than any one person could read, and any narrowing of the field or reduction in the corpus could lead to the suggestion that the geocritic has omitted or overlooked something crucial concerning the particular place that is the object of study. Indeed, Westphal acknowledges that determining a useful corpus would probably require new databases organized around spatial criteria: he argues that, "[t]o find out what real places André Gide represented in his books, reading a good monograph may suffice. However, it will prove less easy to put together a corpus of texts in which the action revolves around the Congo, Chad, or the Vatican" (2011: 117). In addition to innumerable literary works associated with such places, Westphal allows that ostensibly non-literary texts such as tourist brochures or advertising would be suitable for geocritical analysis. Westphal's commitment to the post-modern critique of grand narratives does much to obviate the need for an absolute inclusiveness, which may be a matter of convenience given the wide range of material that could be made available for such an approach.

It should also be clear that my own understanding of geo-criticism differs from Westphal's geocentric approach. As I have tried to show throughout, the spatial turn in literary and cultural studies has opened up new spaces for critical inquiry, in which we may see the ways that writers map their world and readers engage with such literary maps. Geocriticism, broadly conceived, provides a critical theory and practice of spatiality in relation to literature, but Westphal's narrowly geocentric approach fails to encompass the full range of spatial representations stretching from Dostoevsky's "real" St. Petersburg or Faulkner's "fictional" Yoknapatawpha County to Tolkien's "fantastic" Middle-earth, and many more, which also offer important sites for geocritical exploration.

This is partially the reason why geocriticism, broadly under-stood to encompass the analysis of both literary examples of the representations of space and quotidian descriptions of space that appear more generally in the physical and the social sciences, is so timely. Moreover, the increased relocation of the concept of spatiality within the methods and practices we use to make sense of the world in which we live has made clear that mapping is now crucial to a concrete understanding of our being-in-the-world. As Jameson has suggested, "all thinking today is *also*, whatever else it is, an attempt to think the world system as such" (1992: 4), and that thinking involves an indispensable considera-tion of spatiality.

This consideration is not necessarily limited, as we have seen, to the attempts to represent the "real" world or to create more mimetic or accurate maps. Poets and writers help us make sense of the world, but they are not constrained to produce only a realistic portrayal of that world. Similarly, if the critic's task is to help us make sense of the ways we make sense of the world, as Frank Kermode has suggested (1967: 3), then the geocritic or spatially oriented theorist will also wish to move beyond the common-places of quotidian experience. This is a view with which Westphal concurs in his conclusion to *Geocriticism*:

> At a time when literary studies seeks pathways that could lead it out of the merely literary and bring it into line with the related "realities,"

I think geocriticism, insofar as it studies the literary stratifications of referential space, can play an important role, since geocriticism operates somewhere between the geography of the "real" and the geography of the "imaginary" ... two quite similar geographies that may lead to others, which critics should try to develop and explore.

(2011: 170)

In the attempt to think critically about the spaces and places of our own world, we are frequently encouraged to imagine other spaces.

CONCLUSION

OTHER SPACES

Throughout this book, I have been primarily concerned with the literary mapping of real spaces, or, to mention once more the tripartite division of types of space in Edward Soja's theory of spatiality, the mapping of real, imagined, and real-and-imagined spaces. Yet all of these remain situated more or less under the sign of realism, inasmuch as even the fictional or imaginary places are understood to be ways of representing the personal and social spaces of our real world. In this conclusion, however, I want to examine those other spaces which are not usually associated with mimesis, realism, or the real world, but which also maintain a profound influence over literary cartography and geography. In particular, these are the places and spaces presented in the fantastic mode, broadly conceived and encompassing such particular genres as utopia, science fiction, and fantasy. As becomes clear immediately, however, the distinction is rather unstable, oscillatory, and subject to reversals, as the most fantastic literature may also have clear, "real-world" effects, and the most realistic works can often mask the false or misleading truths behind everyday appearances. Fantasy might be all the more useful for thinking about the real spaces of the world. As the British fantasist and theorist China Miéville has pointed out,

> In a fantastic cultural work, the artist pretends that things known to be impossible are not only possible but real, which creates mental space redefining—or pretending to redefine—the impossible. This is sleight of mind, altering the categories of the not-real. Bearing in mind Marx's point that the real and the not-real are constantly cross-referenced in the productive activity by which humans interact with the world, changing the not-real allows one to think differently about the real, its possibilities and its actualities.
>
> (Miéville 2002: 45–46)

Looking at what we might call *otherworldly literature*, I maintain, we also gain a clearer sense of our own "real" world.

As Kathryn Hume has made clear in her impressive study, *Fantasy and Mimesis: Responses to Reality in Western Literature*, the fantastic and the imitative or realistic modes "seem most usefully viewed as the twin impulses behind the creation of literature" (1984: 195). This is not merely a division between representing reality as it really is, and inventing a wholly unreal world. After all, even the most realistic fiction depicts an imaginary world, as we saw in Umberto Eco's meticulously drawn but ultimately fictional Paris in *Foucault's Pendulum*. And even the most *outré* of fantasy worlds will have elements that are recognisable as part of the experience of the reader who can undoubtedly draw vivid connections between the fictional, fantastic space and elements of the everyday world. J.R.R. Tolkien, a founder of the modern fantasy form, once pointed out in a letter to his son, who was serving with the British R.A.F. fighting the Germans during World War II, that the villainous goblin-race, the orcs, are "as real a creation as anything in 'realistic' fiction ... only in real life they are on both sides, of course" (in Carpenter 2000: 82). Thus the overlapping territories of mimesis and fantasy are particularly well suited to a consideration of mapping and spatiality, since the most practical or useful map is fundamentally a fictional or figurative representation of what claims to be a real space.

Mapping itself is very much at home in literatures written or read in a fantastic mode, of course, and many works of fantasy or science fiction include actual maps. Tolkien's *The Hobbit*, which not only includes a map hand-drawn by the author but makes the map itself an essential element of the plot, may be viewed as one of the seminal fantasy novels in this respect. Indeed, in the world *within* a work of fantasy, the reader is encouraged to think of these spaces as being very much real. As Tolkien says elsewhere, "creative Fantasy is founded upon the hard recognition that things are so in the world as it appears under the sun; on a recognition of fact, but not a slavery to it" (2001: 55). In other words, literary cartographies or geographies produced in the fantastic mode are liberated from certain aspects of realism, but they cannot possibly be effective when severed completely from the real world inhabited by readers. This leads to the conclusion that the radical alterity of fantasy is akin to the imaginative projections of a cartographic impulse, reflected in Oedipa Maas's desperate thought in Thomas Pynchon's novel *The Crying of Lot 49*: "Shall I project a world?"

The map and the territory that the map purports to represent are not easily separable. The matter becomes even more difficult in fantasy or science fiction, in which the basic assumptions of referentiality or the willing suspension of disbelief do not always hold. As we observed in the case of the map in Conrad's *Heart of Darkness*, in the everyday world no one *really* thinks that the map reproduces anything other than a representation the figured spaces on its surface, but works of fantasy are permitted to take liberties with common sense. In Lewis Carroll's delightfully bizarre tales of Sylvie and Bruno, for example, the two main characters encounter a foreigner who explains the great advances that his country's cartographers have made in the art and science of mapmaking:

> "What a useful thing a pocket-map is!" I remarked.
>
> "That's another thing we've learned from *your* Nation," said Mein Herr, "map-making. But we've carried it much further than *you*. What would you consider the *largest* map that would be really useful?"
>
> "About six inches to the mile."

"Only *six inches!*" exclaimed Mein Herr. "We very soon got to six *yards* to the mile. Then we tried a *hundred* yards to the mile. And then came the grandest idea of all! We actually made a map of the country, on the scale of *a mile to the mile!*"

"Have you used it much?" I enquired.

"It has never been spread out, yet," said Mein Herr. "The farmers objected: they said it would cover the whole country, and shut out the sunlight. So we now use the country itself, as its own map, and I assure you it does nearly as well."

(Carroll 1893: 169)

Carroll's absurd mapmakers apparently found acolytes in Jorge Luis Borges's (1899–1986) fabled imperial cartographers who "struck a Map of the Empire whose size was that of the Empire, and which coincided point for point with it" (1999: 325). All readers would certainly agree with the judgement of British fantasist Neil Gaiman, in his own variation on the theme, that such a map "would be perfectly accurate and perfectly useless" (2006: xix–xx) for the obvious reason that the space to be mapped is identical with what should be a scaled representation of its contours. However, Gaiman adds an important caveat that is pertinent to any discussion of *literary* geography: "One describes a tale best by telling the tale. ... The tale is the map which is the territory" (xix–xx). Carroll's or Borges's absurdly meticulous mapmakers are in this sense engaging in the literary practice of producing an imaginary world that does in fact overlap point for point with the real world that is the object of its reference. We might also add that this is also true of fictions that claim to be "realistic," where, as in the case of the map in Conrad's novel, the map of the world is represented in terms of imperial allegiances.

As we observed in Chapter 2, the French historian François Hartog has pointed out that the surveyor, as one who maps, is also very much the *rhapsode*, the singer of epic poetry, but also etymologically *one who weaves*; hence, storytelling stitches together different threads, patches, images, and narratives to create something that, while technically a palimpsest or stitched-together ensemble, is itself something new. Gaiman's playful phrase that evaluates maps as "perfectly accurate and perfectly useless" becomes an ironic vision of the role of myth and of spatiality in our lives more generally. From Aristotle's *Poetics* onwards we recall that what distinguishes the poet from other figures is not the use of verse rather than prose, nor does it involve the recounting of facts versus fiction; rather, as Aristotle says, "the poet is a maker of plots." Aristotle's word for "plot" is *mythos*, and perhaps it is no accident that this myth or plot is also a map, a means of plotting a course using a map. Myth is what helps us to see the territory, mapping it as we explore it, and vice versa. Mythic or fantastic cartography thus weaves together a world that is both strangely familiar and utterly novel, bringing together old myths with astonishingly fresh ones to create a world that is also our own world.

It should not be forgotten, perhaps, that there is also an ideological element to mapping, which is made explicit in Conrad's *Heart of Darkness* and elsewhere. In Brian Friel's *Translations*, for instance, the nineteenth-century mapping of Ireland by the English offers an occasion for considering the blending of the mythic with the real, as the indigenous local culture is transformed by the largely linguistic actions—translations and renaming—of the outsiders. This involves the replacing of rich international culture, where the inhabitants can quote the classics, by a much more inferior "English" alternative. Although the dialogue is in English the audience is to imagine that the indigenous inhabitants are speaking Irish or Gaelic. Much of the drama of this play involves the apparently inevitable misunderstandings and mistranslations between the difference cultures, and the presence of actual surveyors and cartographers indicates the extent to which such cultural conflict in bound up in spatial and geographical relations. The overlap of the fantastic or mythic with the real and historical is also not accidental, as a character's rereading of the *Aeneid*, a tale of cultural destruction and renewal, reminds the audience.

Notwithstanding their overlapping aspects, fantastic texts do not perform the exact same function as more realistic texts. Realism at least insists upon conventions that the author and the reader share, and among them is a basic concord regarding reference to quotidian space. To return to the example of Eco's Paris as it appears in *Foucault's Pendulum*, discussed in Chapter 3, although anyone familiar with actual occurrences in Paris may have wondered why Casaubon did not mention the blaze that happened in the "real" neighbourhood on the night of his fictional stroll down the rue Saint-Martin, they would certainly still be able to recognise the general contours of the city itself. Had the reader wondered why Casaubon did not mention the lights of Times Square or the sight of Big Ben, we would know that the reader was mad (or, at least, madder than Eco took him to be). Conversely, what must be acknowledged is the gentlemen's agreement that fantasy readers and their authors have, which allows that the impossible is permitted so long as the genre's formal rules are adhered to. Realistic fiction, even when occasionally depicting unrealistic characters or events, tends to maintain a referential basis.

However, in some respects, the spaces of fantasy do not necessarily or ever coincide with any real place at all. For example, to return to one of the most famous fantasy worlds in modern fiction, Tolkien's Middle-earth, it is clear that the cartography—both the imaginary cartography of Tolkien's narratives and his own literal map made for inclusion in *The Hobbit* and *The Lord of the Rings*—of this imaginary space is essential to the plot. The adventure story and the overall fantasy in *The Hobbit* is established through a largely geographical survey of imaginary places. But, as Tom Shippey has pointed out, most of the toponyms in that novel are really just descriptions (2003: 71). Thus, the Lonely Mountain is a single mountain arising from relatively flat surrounding lands, the Misty Mountains are enshrouded in mist, Mirkwood is a rather murky forest, Rivendell is set in a valley through which a river flows, and Hobbiton is a town of Hobbits. Even the protagonist's home address, Bag End, is itself a joke, whereby Tolkien offers a literal translation of the much posher-sounding French term *cul-de-sac*, thereby poking fun at those members of the Edwardian bourgeoisie who favour the untranslated designation as an indication of their cultural superiority. The generic place-names in *The Hobbit* suggest that its narrative takes place not in a particular, identifiable region, but in some kind of generic space that the knowing reader can recognise. Of course, with the expansive history and geography of *The Lord of the Rings*, which purportedly maintains the same setting as its predecessor, it becomes clear that Tolkien subsequently furnishes his imaginary "otherworld" with immense historical and geographical detail, such that places not only have proper names, but they have names in various languages among different races and over different epochs. Within the fairly limited and mostly circumscribed space of Tolkien's Middle-earth, the imaginary places are accorded almost the same level of reality as many "real" places, of the kind that is to be found in historical romances or medieval literature. For Tolkien, as for many other fantasists, the integrity and roundedness of the world of the novel, with its spaces, its histories, its languages and its inhabitants, are of paramount importance.

This is perhaps why some critics, wary of what seems to be the frivolity or escapism of fantasy as a genre, prefer the more directly applicable images of science fiction or utopia, where the latter is regarded as a corrected version of a "real" world of the reader's experience. Utopia remains both a cartographic enigma and a historical aim, as it refers to a no-place that is also, presumably, a desirable good place: as, for example, in the case of Thomas More's original play on words in the naming of his fanciful island, where both *ou-topos* ("no place") and *eu-topos* ("good place") are simultaneously signified. As Oscar Wilde put it, "A map of the world that does not include Utopia is not worth even glancing at, for it leaves out the one country at which Humanity is always landing. ... Progress is the realization of Utopias" (2001: 241). Utopian literature embodies a fantastic hope for the future or the elsewhere, but it also usually includes an incisive critique of the here and now, as in Samuel Butler's enigmatically named *Erewhon*, a "nowhere" that is also a "now-here," as Deleuze and Guattari observe (1994: 100).

By the mid-twentieth century, utopian discourse, which is also thoroughly political, had been marred by what appeared to be its failures, from the Progressive Movement in the United States to the Soviet Union's communist regime, such that most discussions of "utopia" associated the term with unrealistic hope that could be immediately transformed into dystopias to be found in such works as George Orwell's *Nineteen-Eighty-Four* or Aldous Huxley's *Brave New World*. Orwell's totalitarian nightmare, or Huxley's heavily ironic reference in the title of his novel to a Shakespearean text that recent criticism has itself rendered problematical, represents a fairly conservative response to the claims of Enlightenment scientific and political "progress." Notwithstanding these negative examples, the utopian impulse in theory made possible a critique of the status quo, at least for those pro-utopian novelists like Ursula Le Guin (1929–) or thinkers like the German-American philosopher Herbert Marcuse (1898–1979). Marcuse argued that the aesthetic sphere, and more particularly the power of the imagination, made possible the hope for radical alternatives to the present system, and that fiction could help to both disclose and produce new spaces of liberty for the future. As he put it,

> The truth value of the imagination relates not only to the past but also to the future: the forms of freedom and happiness which it invokes claim to deliver the historical *reality*. In its refusal to accept as final the limitations imposed on freedom and happiness by the reality principle, in its refusal to forget what *can be*, lies the critical function of phantasy.
>
> (Marcuse 1966: 148–49)

But Marcuse adds that "this idea could be formulated without punishment only in the language of art. In the more realistic realm of political theory and even philosophy, it was almost universally defamed as utopian" (150). For Marcuse, literature or the arts more generally can provide the space for imagining alternatives to the status quo. In this view, the maps are not intended to be strictly mimetic representations of existing spaces but imaginative projections of spaces that can be used in people's lives. But this is, after all, what even apparently realistic maps offered; the figured spaces of the map are already utopian in a manner of speaking.

Jameson, whose concept of cognitive mapping is closely associated with his own views on both narrative and utopia, has suggested that utopia is an attempt "to think a system so vast that it cannot be encompassed by the natural or historically developed categories of perception with which human beings normally orient themselves" (1992a: 2). Jameson has elaborated his own utopianism through his discussions of science fiction, a genre he specifically associates with spatiality (see, e.g., 2005: 312–13). It is true that science fiction or utopia or fantasy enable new ways of seeing the spaces of our own world, while also imagining different spaces altogether. In this respect, other-worldly literature and the literary cartography, geography, or geocriticism connected to it, is valuable. As China Miéville has put it, "the fantastic ... is *good to think with*" (2002: 46).

As I noted in Chapter 1, and implicit throughout this book, ways of seeing are themselves historical, and these historically varied methods and interpretations are both the products and the producers of novel ways of imagining the world. As Samuel Y. Edgerton had described, the emergence of linear perspective in Renaissance art and architecture made possible new developments in those fields and also the eventual advances in post-Newtonian physics, space-travel, and atomic energy. Yet Edgerton's "discovered vanishing point" also reveals alternative points of view:

> Surely in some future century, when artists are among those journeying throughout the universe, they will be encountering and endeavoring to depict experiences impossible to understand, let alone render, by the application of a suddenly obsolete linear perspective. It, too, will become "naïve," as they discover new dimensions of visual perception in the eternal, never ultimate, quest to show truth through the art of making pictures.
>
> (Edgerton 1976: 165)

This appropriately fantastic or science-fictional image of new ways of seeing also applies to new ways of telling, and the literary cartography of the future will undoubtedly involve hitherto unforeseeable means of making sense of the world we encounter and of worlds that exist only in the human imagination.

GLOSSARY

Allegory. Retaining its general meaning of a story which tells another story, allegory in spatiality studies may be linked to the figure of the map itself, insofar as the map is a representation of another space, and it is therefore always also allegorical. Moreover, literary cartography might be thought of as allegorical on an additional level, where the presentation of the fictional world becomes a mapping of a referential "real" world. Also, of course, as José Rabasa and others have explored, the actual maps themselves contain a great deal of allegory, whether in their use of seemingly ornamental illustrations or in the conventions used by the mapmaker, such as scale, emphasis, and principles of inclusion or exclusion.

Chronotope. Literally referring to "time-space," the chronotope is a concept developed by Mikhail Bakhtin to make clearer sense of the relations between historical time and geographical space in literature. "In the literary artistic chronotope, spatial and temporal indicators are fused into one carefully thought-out, concrete whole. Time, as it were, thickens, takes on flesh, becomes artistically visible; likewise, space becomes charged and responsive to the movements of time, plot and history" (Bakhtin 1981: 84). For Bakhtin, a historical literary genre maintains its proper chronotope, as in the chronotope of the Greek romance, but a chronotope might also refer to a particular kind of historical space (the *road*, for instance) as it appears in literature.

Cognitive mapping. A practice introduced by Fredric Jameson in his theory of postmodernity. Combining the insights of Kevin Lynch's examination of the "imageability" of cities with Louis Althusser's theory of ideology, Jameson characterizes cognitive mapping as a "practical reconquest of a sense of place" (1991: 51), which would allow the individual subject to locate itself and to represent a seemingly unrepresentable social totality in the postmodern world system.

Core, periphery, semiperiphery. In *The Modern World System*, Immanuel Wallerstein states that "world-economies are divided into core-states and peripheral areas" (1974: 349), with semiperipheral areas or states combining aspects of both. For example, in the nineteenth century, Great Britain and France would be core states, their far-flung colonies in Asia or Africa would be peripheral, and places like Germany or the United States were semiperipheral.

Enlightenment. According to Immanuel Kant, "Enlightenment is mankind's emergence from his self-imposed immaturity" (1963: 3, translation modified). For Kant, the enlightened thinker of the present age had grown up, become an adult, and taken responsibility for his own knowledge, rather than allowing others, such as the medieval Church, to direct and control thinking. Modern science and philosophy, under this view, are made possible by this enlightened perspective. In contrast, the "postmodern condition" (as described by Jean-François Lyotard) is characterized by a mistrust or rejection of the Enlightenment's "grand narratives."

Erdapfel. Created by Martin Behaim in 1492, the "earth-apple" is thought to be the first terrestrial globe, thus marking an advance in the history of cartography.

Existentialism. Broad-based and influential twentieth-century philosophy or theory associated with Martin Heidegger and Jean-Paul Sartre, among others, whose foundation premise is that "existence precedes essence."

Geospace. Term used by Barbara Piatti, among others, to refer to the actual, reference space of the so-called "real world," as distinct from the perceptions or representations of space and from imaginary spaces.

Imageability. In Kevin Lynch's *The Image of the City* (1960), imageability refers to the capacity a given social space, such as a city, has for forming memorable impressions on the minds of its inhabitants. That is, how easily can persons form a useful mental image of the place as they dwell within or move about through the space.

Itinerary. In Michel de Certeau, the itinerary is distinguished from the map. The itinerary refers to the individual's movement through a given space—for example, the pedestrian walking through city streets—while the map presupposes hierarchical or panoptic overview.

Linear perspective. In art, the representation of an image on a flat surface as it would appear to the eye. Linear perspective in art and architecture emerged in the late Middle Ages and the Renaissance, and Leonard Goldstein has argued that it is "a mode of representation specific to capitalism at a particular stage of its development" (1988: 135). Along with the homogenization and quantification of space, linear perspective presupposes an individual observer from whose perspective the imagery is seen.

Mappamundi. From the Latin, "map of the world," this refers to any of a number of medieval European maps (including **T-and-O maps**) that attempt to represent the world. *Mappaemundi* were less useful, and less used, for navigation than **portolan charts**, but were employed as educational or symbolic tools to present classical or religious worldviews.

Mercator projection. A mathematical project developed by cartographer Gerardus Mercator and used in many famous world maps. The Mercator projection solves the dilemma of representing the terraqueous globe's curved space on a flat surface, but it notoriously distorts the images (for example, making Greenland roughly the same size as South America, although the island is really only about one-sixth that size). These maps were useful for navigation, inasmuch as one could more easily plot a course using straight lines. However, as Mark Monmonier has noted, maps using the Mercator projection were sometimes favoured precisely because of the ideological value of the distortions: "The English especially liked the way the Mercator [projection] flattered the British Empire with a central meridian through Greenwich and prominent far-flung colonies in Australia, Canada, and South Africa" (1991: 96).

Mimesis. Representation of reality, particularly referring to "realistic" representations as opposed to fanciful or fantastic images. As Erich Auerbach demonstrated in his *Mimesis*, there are different traditions in Western literature for representing reality.

Nomad/State. Distinction made famous by Gilles Deleuze, describing two different types of space and approaches to space. In *Difference and Repetition*, Deleuze distinguishes between the Cartesian theory of substances that, like the agricultural or statist model, distributes elements of Being by dividing them into fixed categories, demarcating territories and fencing them off from one another, and "a completely other distribution, which must be called nomadic, a nomad *nomos*, without property, enclosure or measure," that does not involve "a division of that which is distributed but rather a division among those who distribute themselves in an open space—a space which is unlimited, or at least without precise limits" (1994: 36). Deleuze goes on to suggest that the nomad and the state have two entirely different types of space associated with them; see **Smooth/ Striated**. The nomad/state distinction also underlies Deleuze's view of the history of philosophy, in which "nomad thinkers" like Lucretius, Spinoza, or Nietzsche emerge in opposition to such "state philosophers" as Descartes or Kant.

Orbis terrarum. Referring to the terrestrial world, the *orbis terrarum* was depicted on medieval T-and-O maps as a circle with a horizontal line across the centre and a vertical line midway through the lower half, completing the *T* and effectively dividing the world into its three continents: Asia, Europe, and Africa. As with other medieval maps, Asia is on top since the orientation of maps was to the East, so Jerusalem represented the centre of the T's crossbar and hence the centre of the world itself.

Orientation. Literally, orientation means "facing east," which is related to the ways that medieval European maps used the Holy Land, specifically Jerusalem, as their primary point of reference. Later the term comes to mean "gain one's bearings" or "understand one's place relative to other places."

Panopticon. The name of the model prison developed by Jeremy Bentham in a 1791 book of that title. The name suggests "seeing all," and the architectural principle is exemplified by its centrally located watchtower, from which could be observed all of the prison cells arranged in a ring around this centre. Hence, the prisoners could be watched at all times and, moreover, are aware of this constant surveillance. In *Discipline and Punish*, Michel Foucault views the panoptic principle as "the utopia of the perfectly governed city" (1977: 198) and a model fo modern societal organization of bodies and spaces.

Portolan chart. In the history of mapmaking, the portolan chart emerged in thirteenth-century Italy and offered remarkably accurate representations of the coastline and of harbours, thus facilitating navigation and travel.

Rhapsode. In ancient Greece and Rome, a rhapsode was a singer of ancient epic poetry, such as those storytellers who would perform the *Iliad* or the *Odyssey*. As the French historian François Hartog has noted, the etymology of the word suggests "weaver," and the storytellers were imagined as sewing together various bits of epic poetry or narrative. Furthermore, in this capacity as a rhapsode or weaver, the storyteller would actually stitch together the disparate parts of the "world" itself (the *oikoumene*), bringing distant places into a cognizable unity. Thus, the rhapsode or storyteller becomes a literary cartographer, surveying, interconnecting, and re-presenting the spaces of the world for the audience.

Smooth/striated. In the spatial philosophy of Gilles Deleuze, these represent two different types of space, associated with the nomad or state respectively; see also **Nomad/state**. Deleuze proposes that nomads have a qualitatively different kind of space from that of the state: "It is the difference between a *smooth* (vectoral, pro-jective, topological) space and a *striated* (metric) space: in the first case 'space is occupied without being counted,' and in the second case 'space is counted in order to be occupied'" (Deleuze and Guattari 1987: 361–62).

Spatial form. As analysed by Joseph Frank in his famous essay, "Spatial Form in Modern Literature" (reprinted in Frank 1991), this refers to the ways that the formal characteristic of works of modern or postmodern literature register a spatiality distinct from or in addition to the temporality of narrative. For example, by estab-lishing a simultaneity of events through the use of juxtaposition or back-and-forth cross-cutting, a narrative may elude its temporal progression and mark its spatiality. Frank argued that the spatial form of modernist novels like James Joyce's *Ulysses* required the reader to project a mental image, not unlike a map, in order to grasp the narrative.

Spatial turn. The increased attention to matters of space, place and mapping in literary and cultural studies, as well as in social theory, philosophy, and other disciplinary fields, since roughly the 1960s. The spatial turn has been analysed and sometimes promoted by Denis Cosgrove, Fredric Jameson, David Harvey, and Edward Soja, among many others.

Spirit of place. Also known as the *genius loci*, the spirit of place originally referred to an actual guardian spirit of a particular place. D.H. Lawrence refers to the spirit of place as a way to understand the particular geographical and cultural characteristics of a local or national literature (1961: 5–6).

Structures of attitude and reference. In *Culture and Imperialism* (1993: 62), Edward Said's conception, drawing upon and expanding Williams's idea of "structures of feeling" (below), used to show how various writers incorporated the effects of empire, sometimes unconsciously, into their works.

Structures of feeling. Raymond Williams's term for the "meanings and values as they are actively lived and felt, and the relations between these and formal or systematic beliefs are in practice variable (including historically variable)" (1977: 132). This is an important conception in Williams's study of the country and the city in British literature, although he later acknowledged that the concept was overly vague.

T-and-O Map: see *Orbis terrarum*.

Thirdspace. Edward Soja's term for the blended, real-and-imagined places, where Firstspace would be the "real" material world and Secondspace would refer to "imagined" representations of space (see Soja 1996: 6).

Topoanalysis. The analysis of places, particularly of those intimate places that make the individual subject what it is, places to which the individual imagination most strongly responds. In *The Poetics of Space* (1964), Gaston Bachelard argues that topoanalysis is a necessary supplement to psychoanalysis.

Utopia. Originally coined by Thomas More as the name of his fictional, ideal society, the word was a pun on the original Greek derivation such that it included a double-meaning of "no place" (*ou-topos*) and "good place" (*eu-topos*).

Wayfinding. From Kevin Lynch's *The Image of the City*, wayfinding refers to practices used by city-dwellers to navigate the urban space, using landmarks and boundaries for guidance.

BIBLIOGRAPHY

Adorno, Theodor W., and Max Horkheimer (1987) *Dialectic of Enlightenment*, New York: Continuum.

Althusser, Louis (1971) "Ideology and Ideological State Apparatuses," in *Lenin and Philosophy and Other Essays*, trans. Ben Brewster, New York: Monthly Review Press.

Anderson, Benedict (1991) *Imagined Communities: Reflections on the Origin and Spread of Nationalism*, rev. edn., London: Verso.

Anderson, Perry (1998) *The Origins of Postmodernity*, London: Verso.

Argan, Giulio Carlos (1964) *The Europe of the Capitals: 1600–1700*, Geneva: Albert Skira.

Auerbach, Erich (1953) *Mimesis: The Representation of Reality in Western Literature*, trans. Willard R. Trask, Princeton: Princeton University Press.

—— (1969) "Philology and *Weltliteratur*," trans. M. and E.W. Said, *Centennial Review* 13 (Winter), 1–17.

—— (2001) *Dante: Poet of the Secular World*, trans. Ralph Manheim, New York: New York Review of Books.

Bachelard, Gaston (1969) *The Poetics of Space*, trans. Maria Jolas, Boston: Beacon Press.

Bakhtin, Mikhail (1981) *The Dialogic Imaginations: Four Essays*, ed. and trans. Caryl Emerson and Michael Holquist, Austin, TX: University of Texas Press.

—— (1984) *Rabelais and His World*, trans. Hélène Iswolsky, Bloomington, IN: Indiana University Press.

Bakhtin, M.M. / Medvedev, P.N. (1978) *The Formal Method of Literary Scholarship*, trans. Albert J. Wehrle, Baltimore: Johns Hopkins University Press.

Baudelaire, Charles (1964) "The Painter of Modern Life," in *The Painter of Modern Life and Other Essays*, ed. and trans. Jonathan Mayne, London: Phaidon Press, 1–40.

Benjamin, Walter (1969) "On Some Motifs in Baudelaire," in *Illuminations*, trans. Harry Zohn, New York: Schocken Books, 155–200.

—— (1978) "A Berlin Chronicle," in *Reflections*, trans. Edmund Jephcott, New York: Harcourt, Brace, Jovanovich, 3–60.

—— (1999) *The Arcades Project*, trans. Howard Eiland and Kevin McLaughlin, Cambridge, MA: Harvard University Press.

Berger, John (1977) *Ways of Seeing*, New York: Penguin.

Berman, Marshall (1982) *All That is Solid Melts into Air: The Experience of Modernity*, New York: Penguin.

Bhabha, Homi, ed. (1990) *Nation and Narration*. London: Routledge.

Bonta, Mark, and John Protevi (2004) *Deleuze and Geophilosophy: A Guide and Glossary*, Edinburgh: University of Edinburgh Press.

Borges, Jorge Luis (1999) "Of Exactitude in Science," in *Collected Fictions*, trans. Andrew Hurley, New York: Penguin.

Braidotti, Rose (2011) *Nomadic Subjects: Embodiment and Sexual Difference in Contemporary Feminist Theory*, Second edn., New York: Columbia University Press.

Braudel, Fernand (1972) *The Mediterranean and the Mediterranean World in the Age of Phillip II*, trans. S. Reynolds, New York: Harper & Row.

Brown, Bill (2005) "The Dark Wood of Postmodernity (Space, Faith, Allegory)," *PMLA* 120.3, 734–50.

Buchanan, Ian, and Gregg Lambert, eds. (2005) *Deleuze and Space*, Edinburgh: Edinburgh University Press.

Buck-Morss, Susan (1990) *The Dialectics of Seeing: Walter Benjamin and the Arcades Project*, Cambridge, MA: MIT Press.

Budgen, Frank (1989) *James Joyce and the Making of* Ulysses, *and Other Writings*, ed. Clive Hart, Oxford: Oxford University Press.

Calvino, Italo (1974) *Invisible Cities*, trans. William Weaver, New York: Harcourt.

—— (2004) *Hermit in Paris: Autobiographical Writings*, trans. Jonathan Cape, New York: Vintage.

Canguillem, Georges (1991) *The Normal and the Pathological*, trans. Carolyn R. Fawcett, New York: Zone Books.

Carpenter, Humphrey, ed. (2000) *The Letters of J.R.R. Tolkien*, Boston: Houghton Mifflin.

Carroll, Lewis (1893) *Sylvie and Bruno Concluded*, London: Macmillan.

Carter, Paul (1987) *The Road to Botany Bay: An Essay in Spatial History*, London: Faber and Faber.

Conley, Tom (1996) *The Self-Made Map: Cartographic Writing in Early Modern France*, Minneapolis, MN: University of Minnesota Press.

Conrad, Joseph (1921) "Geography and Some Explorers," in *Last Essays*, London: J.M. Dent, 1–31.

—— (1969) *Heart of Darkness*, New York: Bantam.

Cosgrove, Denis, ed. (1999) *Mappings*, London: Reaktion Books.

Dante (1984) *The Divine Comedy, Vol. I: Inferno*, trans. Mark Musa, New York: Penguin.

Davis, Mike (1990) *City of Quartz: Excavating the Future in Los Angeles*, London: Verso.

Dear, Michael, Jim Ketchum, Sarah Luria, and Douglas Richardson (2011) *GeoHumanties: Art, History, Text at the Edge of Place*, London: Routledge.

de Certeau, Michel (1984) *The Practice of Everyday Life*, trans. Steven Randall, Berkeley, CA: University of California Press.

Deleuze, Gilles (1977) "Nomad Thought," trans. David Allison, *The New Nietzsche*, ed. David Allison, Cambridge, MA: MIT Press, 142–49.

—— *Foucault* (1988), trans. Séan Hand, Minneapolis, MN: University of Minnesota Press.

—— (1994) *Difference and Repetition*, trans. Paul Patton, New York: Columbia University Press.

Deleuze, Gilles, and Félix Guattari (1980), *Anti-Oedipus*, trans. Mark Seem et al., Minneapolis, MN: University of Minnesota Press.

—— (1987) *A Thousand Plateaus*, trans. Brian Massumi, Minneapolis, MN: University of Minnesota Press.

—— (1994) *What is Philosophy?*, trans. Hugh Tomlinson and Graham Burchell, New York: Columbia University Press.

Deleuze, Gilles, and Claire Parnet, *Dialogues* (1987), trans. Hugh Tomlinson and Barbara Habberjam, New York: Columbia University Press.

Descartes, René (1996) *Meditations on First Philosophy*, ed. J. Cottingham, Cambridge: Cambridge University Press.

Domosh, Mona, and Joni Saeger (2001) *Putting Women in Place: Feminist Geographers Make Sense of the World*, New York: Guilford Press.

Eco, Umberto (1994) *Six Walks in the Fictional Woods*, Cambridge, MA: Harvard University Press.

Edgerton, Samuel Y. (1975) *The Renaissance Rediscovery of Linear Perspective*, New York: Harper and Row.

—— (2009) *The Mirror, the Window, and the Telescope: How Renaissance Linear Perspective Changed Our Vision of the Universe*, Ithaca, NY: Cornell University Press.

Edson, Evelyn (2007) *The World Map, 1300–1492: The Persistence of Tradition and Transformation*, Baltimore: Johns Hopkins University Press.

Foucault, Michel (1965) *Madness and Civilization: A History of Insanity in the Age of Reason*, trans. Richard Howard, New York: Vintage.

—— (1970) *The Order of Things: An Archaeology of the Human Sciences*, trans. anon., New York: Vintage.

—— (1973) *The Birth of the Clinic: An Archaeology of Medical Perception*, trans. A. M. Sheridan Smith, New York: Vintage.

—— (1977) *Discipline and Punish: The Birth of the Prison*, trans. Alan Sheridan, New York: Vintage.

—— (1978) *The History of Sexuality, Volume I: An Introduction*, trans. Robert Hurley, New York: Vintage.

—— (1980a) "The Eye of Power," in *Power/Knowledge: Selected Interviews and Other Writings, 1972–1977*, ed. Colin Gordon, New York: Pantheon, 146–65.

—— (1980b) "Questions on Geography," in *Power/Knowledge: Selected Interviews and Other Writings, 1972–1977*, ed. Colin Gordon, New York: Pantheon, 63–77.

—— (1982) "Space, Knowledge, and Power," in *The Foucault Reader*, ed. Paul Rabinow, New York: Pantheon, 239–56.

—— (1986) "Of Other Spaces," trans. Jay Miskowiec, *Diacritics* 16 (Spring), 22–27.

—— (2006) *History of Madness*, trans. Jean Khalfa, London: Routledge.

Frank, Joseph (1991) *The Idea of Spatial Form*, New Brunswick, NJ: Rutgers University Press.

Freud, Sigmund, and Josef Breuer (2004) *Studies in Hysteria* [1895], trans. N. Luckhurst, New York: Penguin.

Friedrich, Carl J. (1952) *The Age of the Baroque, 1610–1660*, New York: Harper and Row.

Frow, John (2006) *Genre*, London: Routledge.

Gaiman, Neil (2006) *Fragile Things: Short Fictions and Wonders*, New York: Harper-Collins.

Ganser, Alexandra (2009) *Roads of Her Own: Gendered Space and Mobility in American Women's Road Narratives, 1970–2000*, Amsterdam: Rodopi.

Goldstein, Leonard (1988) *The Social and Cultural Roots of Linear Perspective*, Minneapolis, MN: MEP Publications.

Gramsci, Antonio (1971) *Selections from the Prison Notebooks*, eds. and trans. Quentin Hoare and Geoffrey Nowell Smith, New York: International Publishers.

Gregory, Derek (1994) *Geographical Imaginations*, Oxford: Blackwell.

Grosz, Elizabeth (1995) *Space, Time, and Perversion: Essays on the Politics of Bodies*, London: Routledge.

Harley, J.B. (2001) *The New Nature of Maps: Essays in the History of Cartography*, ed. P. Laxon, Baltimore, MD: Johns Hopkins University Press.

Hartog, François (1988) *The Mirror of Herodotus: The Representation of the Other in the Writing of History*, trans. Janet Lloyd, Berkeley: University of California Press.

Harvey, David (1990), *The Condition of Postmodernity: An Enquiry into the Origins of Cultural Change*, Oxford: Blackwell.

Hassan, Ihab (1987) *The Postmodern Turn: Essays on Postmodern Theory and Culture*, Columbus, OH: Ohio State University Press.

Hegel, G.W.F. (1967), *Hegel's Philosophy of Right*, trans. T.M. Knox, Oxford: Oxford University Press.

Heidegger, Martin (1962) *Being and Time*, trans. John Macquarrie and Edward Robinson, New York: Harper and Row.

Hume, Kathryn (1984) *Fantasy and Mimesis: Responses to Reality in Western Literature*, New York: Methuen.

Jameson, Fredric (1971) *Marxism and Form: Twentieth-Century Dialectical Theories of Literature*, Princeton: Princeton University Press.

—— (1981) *The Political Unconscious: Narrative as a Socially Symbolic Act*, Ithaca, NY: Cornell University Press.

—— (1991) *Postmodernism, or, the Cultural Logic of Late Capitalism*, Durham, NC: Duke University Press.

—— (1992a) *The Geopolitical Aesthetic: Cinema and Space in the World System*, Indianapolis, IN, and London: Indiana University Press and the British Film Institute.

—— (1992b) *Signatures of the Visible*, London: Routledge.

—— (1994) *The Seeds of Time*, New York: Columbia University Press.

—— (1998) *The Cultural Turn*, London: Verso.

—— (2005) *Archaeologies of the Future: The Desire Called Utopia and Other Science Fictions*, London: Verso.

—— (2009) *Valences of the Dialectic*, London: Verso.

Kant, Immanuel (1963) "What is Enlightenment?" in *On History*, ed. and trans. Lewis White Beck, Indianapolis, IN: Bobbs-Merrill Company, 3–10.

—— (1992) *Theoretical Philosophy, 1855–1870*, trans. D. Walford and R. Meerbote, Cambridge: Cambridge University Press.

Kermode, Frank (1967) *The Sense of an Ending: Studies in the Theory of Fiction*, Oxford: Oxford University Press.

Kestner, Joseph A. (1978) *The Spatiality of the Novel*, Detroit: Wayne State University Press.

Lawrence, D.H. (1961) *Studies in Classic American Literature*, New York: Vintage.

Lefebvre, Henri (1991) *The Production of Space*, trans. Donald Nicholson-Smith, Oxford: Blackwell.

Lofland, Lyn H. (1973) *A World of Strangers: Order and Action in Urban Public Space*. New York: Basic Books.

Lukács, Georg (1971) *The Theory of the Novel*, trans. Anna Bostock, Cambridge, MA: The MIT Press.

Lynch, Kevin (1960) *The Image of the City*, Cambridge, MA: MIT Press.

Lyotard, Jean-François (1984) *The Postmodern Condition: A Report on Knowledge*, trans. Geoff Bennington and Brian Massumi, Minneapolis, MN: University of Minnesota Press.

MacCabe, Colin (1992a) "Preface," in Fredric Jameson, *The Geopolitical Aesthetic: Cinema and Space in the World System*, Indianapolis, IN, and London: Indiana University Press and the British Film Institute, ix–xvi.

Macherey, Pierre, and Etienne Balibar (1981) "Literature as an Ideological Form," *Praxis* 5, 43–58.

Mandel, Ernst (1975) *Late Capitalism*, trans. Joris de Bres, London: New Left Books.

Marcuse, Herbert (1966) *Eros and Civilization*, Boston: Beacon Press.

Marin, Louis (1984) *Utopics: The Semiological Play of Textual Spaces*, trans. Robert A. Vollrath, Atlantic Highlands, NJ: Humanities Press International.

Marx, Karl (1963) *The Eighteenth Brumaire of Louis Bonaparte*, trans. anon., New York: International Publishers.

Marx, Karl, and Friedrich Engels (1998) *The Communist Manifesto*, trans. anon., New York: Signet.

Massey, Doreen (1994) *Space, Place, and Gender*, Minneapolis, MN: University of Minnesota Press.

Mather, Cotton (1862) *The Wonders of the Invisible World*, London: John Russell Smith.

Miéville, China (2002) "Editorial Introduction," *Symposium: Marxism and Fantasy*, in *Historical Materialism* 10.4, 39–49.

Melville, Herman (1988) *Moby-Dick, or, The Whale*, eds. Harrison Hayford, Hershel Parker, and G. Thomas Tanselle, Evanston and Chicago: Northwestern University Press and the Newberry Library.

Mitchell, Peta (2008) *Cartographic Strategies of Postmodernity: The Figure of the Map in Contemporary Theory and Fiction*, London: Routledge.

—— (2011) "'The stratified record upon which we set out feet': The Spatial Turn and the Multi-Layering of History, Geography, and Geology," in Dear et al., *GeoHumanties*, 71–83.

Monmonier, Mark (1991) *How to Lie with Maps*, Chicago: University of Chicago Press.

Moretti, Franco (1983) "The Soul and the Harpy," trans. by David Forgacs, in *Signs Taken for Wonders: On the Sociology of Literary Forms*, London: Verso, 1–41.

—— (1996) *Modern Epic: The World-System from Goethe to García Márquez*, trans. Quentin Hoare, London: Verso.

—— (1998) *Atlas of the European Novel, 1800–1900*, London: Verso.

—— (2000a) "Conjectures on World Literature," *New Left Review* 1, (January–February), 54–68.

—— (2000b) "The Slaughterhouse of Literature," *Modern Language Quarterly* 61.1 (March), 207–27.

—— (2005) *Graphs, Maps, Trees: Abstract Models for a Literary History*, London: Verso.

—— (2006) *The Novel*, 2 vols., ed. Franco Moretti, Princeton: Princeton University Press.

Mumford, Lewis (1938) *The Culture of Cities*, New York: Harcourt, Brace, and Co.

Olson, Charles (1947) *Call Me Ishmael*, San Francisco: City Lights.

—— (1973) "Notes for the Proposition: Man is Prospective," *boundary 2: A Journal of Post-Modernism* 2:1/2 (Autumn), 1–6.

Padrón, Ricardo (2004) *The Spacious Word: Cartography, Literature, and Empire in Early Modern Spain*, Chicago: University of Chicago Press.

—— (2007) "Mapping Imaginary Worlds," in *Maps: Finding Our Place in the World*, ed. James R. Akerman and Robert W. Karrow Jr., Chicago: University of Chicago Press, 255–87.

Perec, Georges (2010) *An Attempt at Exhausting a Place in Paris*, trans. Marc Lowenthal, Cambridge, MA: Wakefield Press.

Piatti, Barbara (2008) *Die Geographie der Literatur: Schauplätze, Handlungsräume, Raumphantasien*, Göttingen: Wallstein Verlag.

Proust, Marcel (1981) *In Search of Lost Time*, trans. C.K. Scott Moncreiff et al. New York: Random House.

Pynchon, Thomas (1966) *The Crying of Lot 49*, New York: Harper and Row.

Rabasa, José (1993) *Inventing America: Spanish Historiography and the Formation of Eurocentrism*, Norman, OK: University of Oklahoma Press.

Ray, Christopher (1991) *Time, Space, and Philosophy*, London: Routledge.

Rodaway, Paul (1994) *Sensuous Geographies: Body, Sense, and Place*, London: Routledge.

Rose, Gillian (1993) *Feminism and Geography: The Limits of Geographical Knowledge*, Minneapolis, MN: University of Minnesota Press.

Ross, Kirsten (1988) *The Emergence of Social Space: Rimbaud and the Paris Commune*, Minneapolis, MN: University of Minnesota Press.

Russell, Bertrand (2004) *The History of Western Philosophy*, London: Routledge.

Said, Edward (1978) *Orientalism*, New York: Vintage.

—— (1993) *Culture and Imperialism*, New York: Knopf.

Sartre, Jean-Paul (1956) *Being and Nothingness: A Phenomenological Essay on Ontology*, trans. Hazel E. Barnes, New York: Washington Square Press.

—— (2004) *The Imaginary: A Phenomenological Psychology of the Imagination*, trans. Jonathan Webber, London: Routledge.

—— (2007) *Existentialism is a Humanism*, trans. Carol Macomber, New Haven: Yale University Press.

Sassen, Saskia (1991) *The Global City: New York, London, Tokyo*, Princeton: Princeton University Press.

Shippey, Tom (2003) *The Road to Middle-earth*, Boston: Houghton Mifflin.

Simmel, Georg (1950) "The Metropolis and Mental Life," in *The Sociology of Georg Simmel*, ed. and trans. Kurt H. Wolff, New York: The Free Press, 409–24.

Soja, Edward W. (1989) *Postmodern Geographies: The Reassertion of Space in Critical Social Theory*, London: Verso.

—— (1996) *Thirdspace: Journeys to Los Angeles and Other Real-and-Imagined Places*, Oxford: Blackwell.

Sontag, Susan (1977) *On Photography*, New York: Farrar, Strauss, and Giroux.

Steiner, George (1976) *Extraterritorial: Papers on Literature and the Language of Revolution*, New York: Atheneum.

Tally, Robert T. (1996) "Jameson's Project of Cognitive Mapping: A Critical Engagement," in Rolland G. Paulston, ed., *Social Cartography: Mapping Ways of Seeing Social and Educational Change*, New York: Garland, 399–416.

—— (2009) *Melville, Mapping and Globalization: Literary Cartography in the American Baroque Writer*, London: Continuum.

——, ed. (2011) *Geocritical Explorations: Space, Place, and Mapping in Literary and Cultural Studies*, New York: Palgrave Macmillan.

Tolkien, J.R.R. (2001) *Tree and Leaf*, New York: HarperCollins.

Tuan, Yi-Fu (1977) *Space and Place: The Perspective of Experience*, Minneapolis, MN: University of Minnesota Press.

Turchi, Peter (2004) *Maps of the Imagination: The Writer as Cartographer*, San Antonio, TX: Trinity University Press.

Wallerstein, Immanuel (1974) *The Modern World-System*. 3 vols. New York: Academic Press.

Wegner, Phillip E. (2002a) *Imaginary Communities: Utopia, the Nation, and the Spatial Histories of Modernity*, Berkeley, CA: University of California Press.

—— (2002b) "Spatial Criticism: Critical Geography, Space, Place, and Textuality," in *Introducing Criticism at the 21st Century*, ed. Julian Wolfreys, Edinburgh: Edinburgh University Press, 179–201.

—— (2009) *Life Between Two Deaths: U.S. Culture in the Long Nineties*, Durham, NC: Duke University Press.

Westphal, Bertrand (2011) *Geocriticism: Real and Fictional Spaces*, trans. R. Tally, New York: Palgrave Macmillan.

Wilde, Oscar (2001) "The Soul of Man Under Socialism," in *The Soul of Man Under Socialism and Selected Critical Prose*, ed. Linda Dowling, New York: Penguin.

Williams, Raymond (1973) *The Country and the City*, Oxford: Oxford University Press.

—— (1976) *Keywords*, Oxford: Oxford University Press.

—— (1977) *Marxism and Literature*, Oxford: Oxford University Press.

—— (1981) *Politics and Letters: Interviews with* New Left Review, London: Verso.

Wolf, Eric R. (1997) *Europe and the People Without History*, Berkeley, CA: University of California Press.

Wood, Denis (1992) *The Power of Maps*, New York: Guilford Press.

Woolf, Virginia (1977) "Literary Geography," in *Books and Portraits: Some Further Selections from the Literary and Biographical Writings of Virginia Woolf*, ed. Mary Lyon, New York: Harcourt, Brace, Jovanovitch, 158–61.

INDEX

Theory After 'Theory'

Edited by **Jane Elliott** and **Derek Attridge**

This volume argues that theory, far from being dead, has undergone major shifts in order to come to terms with the most urgent cultural and political questions of today. Offering an overview of theory's new directions, this groundbreaking collection includes essays on affect, biopolitics, biophilosophy, the aesthetic, and neoliberalism, as well as examinations of established areas such as subaltern studies, the postcolonial, and ethics.

Influential figures such as Agamben, Badiou, Arendt, Deleuze, Derrida and Meillassoux are examined in a range of contexts. Gathering together some of the top thinkers in the field, this volume not only speculates on the fate of theory but shows its current diversity, encouraging conversation between divergent strands. Each section places the essays in their contexts and stages a comparison between different but ultimately related ways in which key thinkers are moving beyond poststructuralism.

Contributors: Amanda Anderson, Ray Brassier, Adriana Cavarero, Eva Cherniavsky, Rey Chow, Claire Colebrook, Laurent Dubreuil, Roberto Esposito, Simon Gikandi, Martin Hägglünd, Peter Hallward, Brian Massumi, Peter Osborne, Elizabeth Povinelli, William Rasch, Henry Staten, Bernard Stiegler, Eugene Thacker, Cary Wolfe, Linda Zerilli.

2011: 234x156: 336pp
Hb: 978-0-415-48418-3
Pb: 978-0415-48419-0
eBook: 978-0-203-83116-8